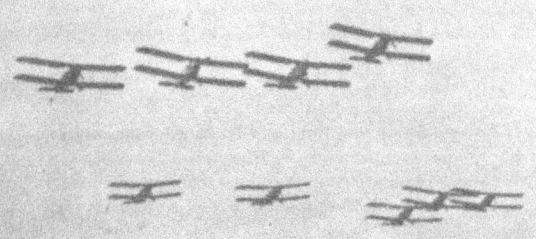

CONTENTS

Roland Garros: The Man Who Put Wings on War by Arch Whitehouse.... 5
Werner Voss: Pride of the Hussars by William E. Barrett.............. 17
Georges Guynemer: The Fragile Knight by William E. Barrett......... 35
Raoul Lufbery: Ace of the Lafayette by William W. Walker........... 47
Edward Mannock: The Crippled Eagle by William E. Barrett.......... 65
René Fonck: The Stork Who Sought Glory by William E. Barrett...... 79
Ernst Udet: Duel Master of the Sky by Richard Hanser............... 91
William Barker: Greatest Pilot the World Has Known by William W. Walker 105
Frank Luke: Balloon Buster by William E. Barrett.................. 117
Elliott White Springs: The War Bird Who'll Never Die by William E. Barrett 131

The photographs that appear in SKY FIGHTERS OF WORLD WAR I are from the collection of WILLIAM E. BARRETT, noted novelist, aeronautical historian and contributor to this volume.

Bristol Aeroplane Company, Ltd.

INTRODUCTION

Ever since CAVALIER Magazine first began publishing World War I aviation stories, the editors have almost daily received requests for an anthology which would have as its subject the great aces of the first great war.

Here, through the courtesy of Fawcett Books, is just such a volume.

The popularity of the CAVALIER series raises an interesting question. What is the reason for the great resurgence of interest in this phase of that long-ago war?

Perhaps the greatest appeal lies in the way these men fought and died. Their true-to-life stories defy the fiction writer to improve on them. Who could create a character like Micky Mannock or Frank Luke or Elliott White Springs? What death scene could be more thrilling than that witnessed by men on the western front on the day that Werner Voss went west? Who could conjure up that fight of Billy Barker's the day he tackled 60 German planes—singlehanded? Who would dare end a story the way Guynemer's story ends, the way that French school children are told about him to this day, that "one day he flew so high he could never come down."

There is also an appeal here that is easier to appreciate than it is to explain. The "sky fighters" of World War I arouse nostalgia because they were the last of their kind; the last cavaliers, the last gallants of war. Although they constantly lived with the threat of death, they could carry on the pretense that it was all a game played with a set of rules that only they could understand. Their presence in the air made them all part of a brotherhood temporarily split into factions by the harsh circumstances of war.

Consider the anachronistic if chivalrous actions seen in what was otherwise a ruthless war—Guynemer pulling his guns off target when he sees that Udet's guns are jammed; Boelcke spending long hours in prison camps and hospitals with his surviving victims; the Royal Air Force declaring their own private armistice to come and pay respects to the dead Richthofen.

Whatever it is that you like about World War I aviation—the fascination of primitive flying machines, the individuality of the first sky fighters or the knighthood of the air—we believe you'll find it in this book. The staff of CAVALIER is proud to be able to help shed light on that first epochal struggle for command of the sky.

—Bob Curran, Editor, CAVALIER Magazine

Drawings by EDWARD A. KNAPP

IT TAKES A REAL MAN TO WIN AN I.C.S. DIPLOMA!

Here's training for the man who can take it "straight"—without the fancy trimmings.

With I.C.S., your "classroom" is your home. Your "laboratory" or "shop" is the place you work. Every minute you spend is productive—no commuting, no long-winded discussion groups, no waiting for slower students to catch up.

You gauge your progress not by marks and grades alone but by pay boosts and promotions. And these are likely to come fast.

This is the most demanding kind of training. You select your own subjects, set your own pace, apply what you learn to your own specific needs —all while holding down a full-time job and possibly supporting a family.

Is it any wonder that men who can win I.C.S. diplomas often turn out to be leaders in their fields? I.C.S. has more of its former students now in supervisory and management positions than any other school.

It takes a real man to win an I.C.S. diploma. And the first step is mailing the coupon. Such a simple act sounds easy. Actually, it's the one thing that separates the "planners" from the "plodders." If you're the man we think you are, you'll mail the coupon NOW.

For Real Job Security—Get an I. C. S. Diploma!   I. C. S., Scranton 15, Penna.   Accredited Member, National Home Study Council

---

INTERNATIONAL CORRESPONDENCE SCHOOLS — ICS

BOX 97144F, SCRANTON 15, PENNA.   (In Hawaii, reply P.O. Box 418, Honolulu)   (Partial list of courses)

Without cost or obligation, send me "HOW to SUCCEED" and the opportunity booklet about the field BEFORE which I have marked X (plus sample lesson):

ARCHITECTURE and BUILDING CONSTRUCTION
- ☐ Air Conditioning
- ☐ Architecture
- ☐ Arch. Drawing and Designing
- ☐ Building Contractor
- ☐ Building Estimator
- ☐ Carpenter Builder
- ☐ Carpentry and Millwork
- ☐ Heating
- ☐ Painting Contractor
- ☐ Plumbing
- ☐ Reading Arch. Blueprints

ART
- ☐ Commercial Art
- ☐ Magazine Illus.
- ☐ Sign Painting and Design'g
- ☐ Sketching and Painting

AUTOMOTIVE
- ☐ Automobile
- ☐ Auto Body Rebuilding and Refinishing
- ☐ Auto Engine Tuneup
- ☐ Auto Electrical Technician
- ☐ Diesel Engines

AVIATION
- ☐ Aero-Engineering Technology
- ☐ Aviation Engine Mech.
- ☐ Reading Aircraft Blueprints

BUSINESS
- ☐ Accounting
- ☐ Advertising
- ☐ Bookkeeping and Cost Accounting
- ☐ Business Administration
- ☐ Business Management
- ☐ Clerk Typist
- ☐ Creative Salesmanship
- ☐ Managing a Small Business
- ☐ Professional Secretary
- ☐ Public Accounting
- ☐ Purchasing Agent
- ☐ Real Estate Salesmanship
- ☐ Salesmanship
- ☐ Salesmanship and Management
- ☐ Traffic Management

CHEMICAL
- ☐ Analytical Chemistry
- ☐ Chemical Engineering
- ☐ Chem. Lab. Technician
- ☐ General Chemistry

- ☐ Oil Field Technology
- ☐ Pulp and Paper Making

CIVIL ENGINEERING
- ☐ Civil Engineering
- ☐ Construction Engineering
- ☐ Highway Engineering
- ☐ Professional Engineer (Civil)
- ☐ Reading Struc. Blueprints
- ☐ Sanitary Engineer
- ☐ Sewage Plant Operator
- ☐ Structural Engineering
- ☐ Surveying and Mapping
- ☐ Water Works Operator

DRAFTING
- ☐ Aircraft Drafting
- ☐ Architectural Drafting
- ☐ Drafting & Machine Design
- ☐ Electrical Drafting
- ☐ Electrical Engineer Drafting
- ☐ Industrial Piping Drafting
- ☐ Mechanical Drafting
- ☐ Sheet Metal Drafting

ELECTRICAL
- ☐ Electrical Appliance Servicing
- ☐ Electrical Engineering

- ☐ Electric Motor Repairman
- ☐ Elec. Engr. Technician
- ☐ Elec. Light and Power
- ☐ Practical Electrician
- ☐ Practical Lineman
- ☐ Professional Engineer

HIGH SCHOOL
- ☐ Good English
- ☐ High School Diploma
- ☐ High School General
- ☐ H. S. College Prep. (Eng'r'g & Science)
- ☐ High School Math
- ☐ High School Science
- ☐ Short Story Writing

LEADERSHIP
- ☐ Industrial Foremanship
- ☐ Industrial Supervision
- ☐ Personnel-Labor Relations
- ☐ Supervision

MECHANICAL and SHOP
- ☐ Diesel Engines
- ☐ Gas-Elec. Welding
- ☐ Heating and Air Conditioning
- ☐ Industrial Engineering
- ☐ Industrial Instrumentation

- ☐ Industrial Safety
- ☐ Machine Shop Practice
- ☐ Mechanical Engineering
- ☐ Plumbing and Heating
- ☐ Professional Engineer
- ☐ Quality Control
- ☐ Reading Shop Blueprints
- ☐ Refrigeration and Air Conditioning
- ☐ Tool Design ☐ Tool Making

RADIO, TELEVISION
- ☐ General Electronics Tech.
- ☐ Industrial Electronics
- ☐ Practical Radio-TV Eng'r'g
- ☐ Radio-TV Servicing
- ☐ TV Technician

RAILROAD
- ☐ General Railroad

STEAM and DIESEL POWER
- ☐ Combustion Engineering
- ☐ Power Plant Engineer
- ☐ Stationary Diesel Engr.
- ☐ Stationary Steam Engines

TEXTILE
- ☐ General

Name_____ Age____ Home Address_____

City_____ Zone____ State_____ Working Hours_____ A.M. to P.M._____

Occupation_____

Canadian residents send coupon to International Correspondence Schools, Canadian, Ltd., Montreal, Canada.... Special low monthly tuition rates to members of the U. S. Armed Forces.

Sky Fighters of WORLD WAR I

A FAWCETT BOOK	NUMBER 484
LARRY EISINGER	EDITOR-IN-CHIEF
GEORGE TILTON	MANAGING EDITOR
SILVIO LEMBO	ART EDITOR

W. H. Fawcett, Jr. . . . . President
Roger Fawcett . . . . General Manager
Donald P. Hanson . . . Assistant General Manager
Gordon Fawcett . . . . Secretary-Treasurer
Roscoe Fawcett . . . . Circulation Director
Ralph Daigh . . . . Editorial Director
James B. Boynton . . . . . Advertising Director
Al Allard . . . . Art Director
Ralph Mattison . . . . . Associate Art Director
George H. Carl . . . . Production Director

W. STEVENSON BACON   EDITOR

Staff Artists
NICK CARLUCCI . . . . ASSOCIATE ART EDITOR
Harold E. Price   •   Michael Gaynor
Larry Flanagan   •   John S. Selvaggio
Bob Vatter   •   Bill Muccio
Ed Kaplan   •   Richard LaMonaca
Richie Rhodes

Phyllis J. Bendremer . . . . Production Editor
Benita Rockwood . . . Assistant Production Editor

SKY FIGHTERS OF WORLD WAR I, Fawcett Book 484, is published by Fawcett Publications, Inc., Greenwich, Connecticut. Editorial and Advertising Offices: 67 West 44th Street, New York 36, New York. General Offices: Fawcett Building, Greenwich, Connecticut. Printed in U.S.A. Copyright 1961 by Fawcett Publications, Inc.

Bristols of 139 Squadron, R.A.F., on patrol over the Alps, July 1918. The Bristol Fighter was so successful under the hazardous conditions along the Italian frontier that a full squadron was requested. William G. Barker was promoted to major and given command.

Cover painting by JO KOTULA

The pilot featured on our cover is the great ace duelist of World War I, Oberleutnant Ernst Udet, flying his pet Fokker D-7. The French pilot at the controls of the Spad 13 must be well aware of his opponent's identity, as the red and white striped upper wing of the Fokker flaunted a challenge from a great distance. The lower wing was painted in the printed lozenge-camouflage pattern now familiar to World War I buffs.

On the flippers, Udet painted his famous nose-thumbing legend, "Du doch nicht," meaning "but not you!" and many an Allied pilot lived but a few moments after getting close enough to read this derisive admonition.—Jo Kotula

Roland Garros
The Man Who Put Wings on War

By Arch Whitehouse

THAT day in 1914 when the Germans declared war with a running start, the better part of the French "air force" was being wined and dined in Berlin. His name was Roland Garros, and along with being one of the great stunt pilots of all time, he had one of those ebullient natures completely uninhibited by common sense. He was also something of a phenomenon in that he was an accomplished artist, a piano virtuoso, a singer and dancer of Paris music hall merit, and for all that he was of the lean and vibrant type, a drinker of astounding capacity. Setting him still further apart from the common herd, he was wealthy.

But on this evening of August 3, he was in serious trouble, and he knew it. For three weeks he had been making exhibition flights over the German capital in his tiny Morane-Saulnier with such spectacular results that his front-page publicity had all but crowded out the ominous rumors of war. Every day a new triumph, and every night a new round of banquets for the dashing French aeronaut. And now, through a pink cloud of champagne bubbles, and surrounded by German officers who had gone wild at the announcement of war, he saw himself as a fat and glossy sucker of enormous size. In glorifying the French aeronaut, the Germans had done a magnificent job of lulling suspicion in Paris. He, Roland Garros, had been the decoy that had drawn attention elsewhere while the German Army massed for its drive.

The champagne was flowing freely, and he had no trouble intercepting a bottle with which to collect his thoughts. But certainly, the Germans had played him for a hero to demonstrate that they had nothing but admiration for the French. And in that case, as a big cog in their plans, it was not likely they would ship him and his plane back to Paris with their best wishes. More likely he would win the distinction of being the first French prisoner of the war, as indeed he already was. But if the Germans knew what he had in store for them, he would have been guarded by a regiment.

In the course of time and drinking Garros made a perfectly natural request, indicating with Gallic realism that his back teeth were afloat. Roaring with laughter, the Germans hoisted him to his feet, steadied him, and then pointed him in the direction of the men's room. When next they were to see him again, it would be after he had all but cleared the skies of German planes, for this was *the* Roland Garros, first knight of the air, first ace, and first to put wings on sudden death.

In his own account of his escape, Garros made light of it, but for sheer, crazy daring it belongs with the classics. When he reached the men's room the window was open, as well

American Press Association

it should be on a hot August night, and he kept right on going. Because of the publicity, with his pictures in all the papers and magazines, he dared not risk a taxi or exposure on a lighted street, but with his airman's picture of Berlin to guide him, he was able to make his way through a labyrinth of alleys and back streets like a native-born street urchin. His goal was an exhibition field on the outskirts of the city where his plane was hangared in a tent, and he arrived there shortly after midnight.

He knew his plane was guarded night and day by a squad of soldiers, technically to protect it from avid souvenir hunters, but now he knew the guard was there to see that the French plane did not leave the country. He approached boldly but with a drunken stagger, his one idea being that if the guards on the midnight-to-dawn shift were reasonably human, they would not be averse to a liberal supply of schnapps with which to celebrate the declaration of war. As it turned out, the guards had themselves reached that same conclusion before his arrival and had transferred their lonesome vigil to a nearby beerhall.

In the light of aviation history, the defection of the guards was more of a technicality than an actuality, and certainly they had no way of knowing that Garros was to write a

Roland Garros, famous as a pilot before the war, was determined to carry the conflict into the clouds. Consequently, he became the first man to fire a machine gun through the propeller arc, clearing the skies of German planes. Unfortunately, he literally shot himself down behind German lines when the constant hammering of bullets against the steel deflector plates on his prop knocked the engine out of balance, thus causing a forced landing. He later escaped, but was killed in the air on October 5, 1918.

new kind of history on his own that night.

In the first place, pilots did not fly at night in 1914. With no instruments to provide an artificial horizon, the few pilots who had tried it had left an awful lot of wreckage behind to prove that moonlight was elusive stuff. In the second place, the best of flying fields were of a rudimentary order, and the Berlin exhibition field was of a lower order than that. Along with the regulation assortment of furrows, chuckholes, stumps, and rocks, it was closely surrounded by buildings, trees, and high-tension wires, and a belief had grown up that a pilot should have a clear view of such impedimenta before taking off. And in the third place (with many more "places" still available) it took eight men to crank up a plane—three on each side to hold down the wings, a strong idiot to swing the propeller and the pilot to work the priming pump.

One of the features of the Le Rhône rotary engine that powered Garros' tiny single-seater was that it had no idling speed. When it took hold, it was bang-on all the way, and even the six men anchoring the wings had trouble restraining its enthusiasm.

Thus, there was little danger that Garros would attempt a night flight or that he could manage it if he should. The unguarded plane was perfectly safe.

In the pitch-darkness of the tent, Garros gassed up his plane from cans of "essence," stopping only when the overflow gave his orange-crate fuselage all the makings of a grand torch. The fumes, in the hot confines of the tent, had added a certain giddiness to the champagne that continued to bubble delightfully in his nose. He pushed his plane out into the night air, feeling no strain. As a matter of fact, even when fully gassed, his plane weighed no more than a modern highway cop's motorcycle, and packed about half the power.

G arros dragged his plane along to his usual starting place, and aimed it in a direction freer than most of obstacles. Fortunately the night was calm, so wind was not one of his worries. In the cockpit he jiggled a few things, muttered some appropriate incantations, tripped over a guy wire and fell back to the ground.

Now he had to swing the prop. If he stood in front and the motor took hold, the plane would leap over him with the prop slicing him into salami on the way. So he had to stand on the side, pull, and hope the second blade didn't split his head on the follow-through. He pulled.

There was a roar. The wing of the monoplane caught him in the midriff, draping him over the leading edge like a fluttering towel. He pulled himself up on a handful of wires.

Garros' secret weapon, German version: This is the same type of metal deflector mounted on the propeller that Garros used on his Morane to fire through the prop, but the installation is German and the machine gun is the Spandau.

ROLAND GARROS

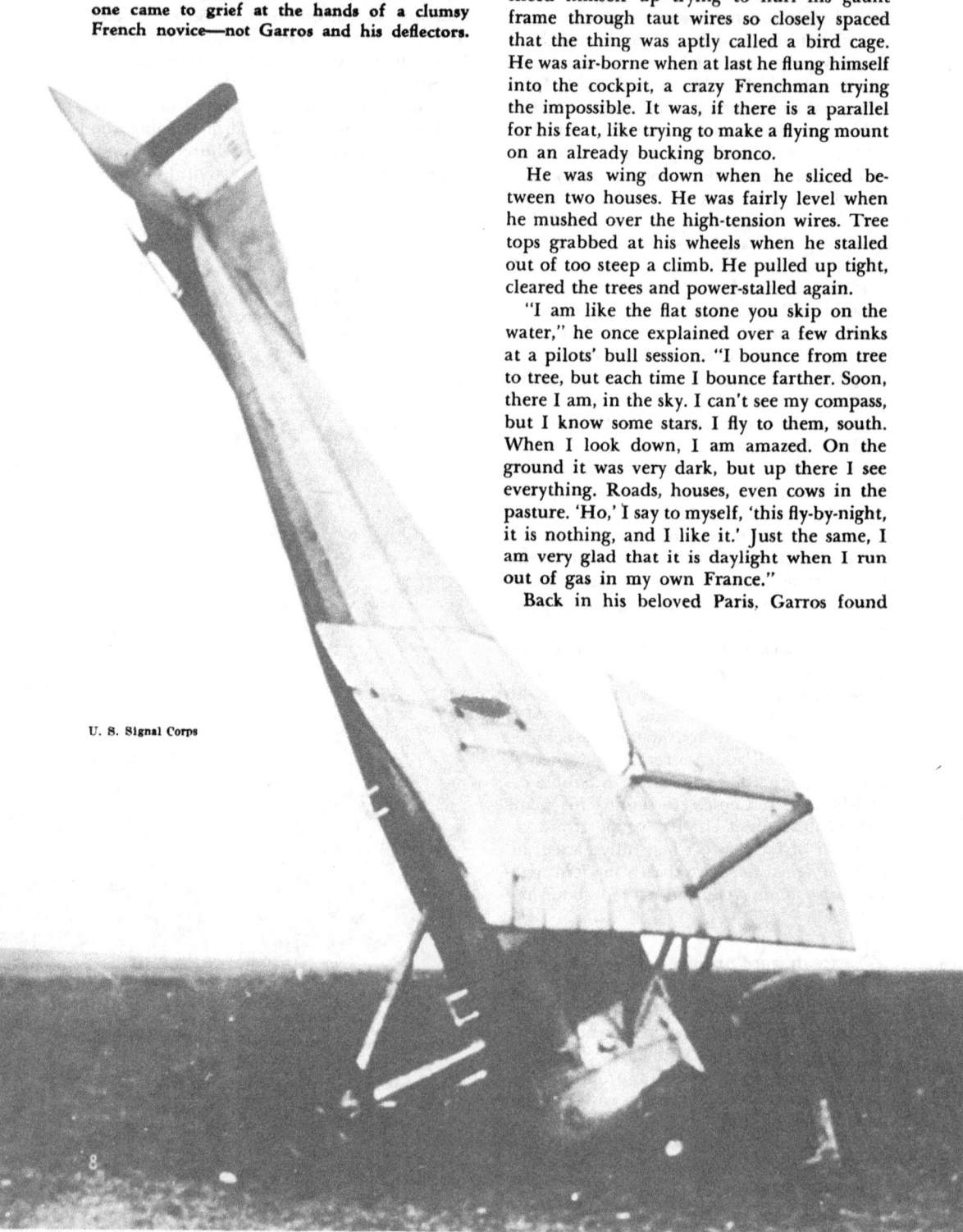

A Morane Parasol, similar to the plane on which Garros installed his deflectors. The Parasol ultimately became a school ship, and this one came to grief at the hands of a clumsy French novice—not Garros and his deflectors.

U. S. Signal Corps

Beneath him the plane was bucking, pitching, gaining speed, and trying to ground-loop. He sliced himself up trying to hurl his gaunt frame through taut wires so closely spaced that the thing was aptly called a bird cage. He was air-borne when at last he flung himself into the cockpit, a crazy Frenchman trying the impossible. It was, if there is a parallel for his feat, like trying to make a flying mount on an already bucking bronco.

He was wing down when he sliced between two houses. He was fairly level when he mushed over the high-tension wires. Tree tops grabbed at his wheels when he stalled out of too steep a climb. He pulled up tight, cleared the trees and power-stalled again.

"I am like the flat stone you skip on the water," he once explained over a few drinks at a pilots' bull session. "I bounce from tree to tree, but each time I bounce farther. Soon, there I am, in the sky. I can't see my compass, but I know some stars. I fly to them, south. When I look down, I am amazed. On the ground it was very dark, but up there I see everything. Roads, houses, even cows in the pasture. 'Ho,' I say to myself, 'this fly-by-night, it is nothing, and I like it.' Just the same, I am very glad that it is daylight when I run out of gas in my own France."

Back in his beloved Paris, Garros found

himself more of a hero there than he had been in Berlin. In the strange confusion that accompanies the start of a war, Berlin newspapers had continued to arrive with German regularity, and they had been unanimous in denouncing his night flight. Along with calling him a thief for stealing his own plane, they who had used him as a decoy now claimed he had planned his whole exhibition tour in order to take aerial photographs of every fortress in Germany, including the palace of Kaiser Wilhelm himself. It was not exactly a legitimate complaint, fortresses and palaces being among the most photographed places in Germany by tourists from all nations, but it did serve to relieve some of the anger Garros felt at being used for a sucker.

Nevertheless, Garros could not forgive the Germans for what he considered a personal betrayal, and he was aching for revenge. It did not seem likely he would get it. A roll call of all the flying machines in France in August 1914 turned up only 136, of which about 100 deserved the title by courtesy only. Of the pilots, about half were rich dilettantes who had taken up flying as a sport with high female appeal. A quarter were professional barnstormers who provided thrills and hopped passengers for a precarious living, and the rest were designers, inventors, and mechanics who could not stay out of the air for love or money. There was not a warrior in the lot, nor was there anyone from top brass to company cook who thought of the flying machine as anything more than a roving observation platform. Except for Garros, that is. He wanted to fly his plane over Berlin and fire his pistol into the crowds below just to get even.

For observation purposes the French did organize the Morane-Saulnier Escadrille No. 23, and grabbed what pilots it could, foremost among them being Garros. The outfit was a bit on the unconventional side, cognac being considered an essential part of the training diet, but that would have been all right if it were not for the infantry officers placed in charge. To prepare the men for the air, they were subjected day after day to close order drill, some remarkably effective training in the use of the saber, and all the inside dope on personal defense in the midst of a cavalry charge. "Hamstring the horses," they were advised.

In the meantime the Germans were within 50 miles of Paris, with German observation planes doing a magnificent job of finding routes defended only by peasants with pitchforks. In desperation, and in spite of the dire warnings of the infantry officer that his pilots were still several months, if not years, short of being soldiers, the pilots were turned loose to see what the Germans were doing. Among them were such men as Adolphe Pégoud, the first barnstormer to loop-the-loop; Eugene Gilbert and Marc Pourpe, who could fly anything with wings; Vedrines, the great designer, and Garros.

Garros was the wild one. There are scores of stories to testify to the fact that during the first months of the war the pilots of both sides thought their lives to be in sufficient jeopardy just being in the air, and that any additional risks, like being shot at, were constitutionally unfair and definitely undesirable. It is a matter of record that German pilots on their way to scout the French ground forces would wave salutes to French pilots on their way to scout the German infantry, and vice versa. The air was a vast neutral territory, and the airmen in it were all members of a big, happy family forced by circumstance to serve different masters.

Garros did not share that attitude. To him the Germans invading his France and threatening his favorite Montmartre boîte de nuit, whether they be on foot, in trucks, or in the air, were just so many Huns to be killed, and he was eager to get on with his self-appointed task. Instead of waving a salute he waved a pistol and always felt frustrated when his bullets fell short.

After several such futile efforts, he began to realize he was the victim of an illusion. An oncoming plane, seen through the blades of his propeller, presented a relatively stable target, while he himself felt as though he were standing still. But when the oncoming plane cleared the edge of his propeller, giving him an unobstructed shot, it went flashing by faster than he could shoot at it. He was not standing still at all, but spurting through the air at 80 mph, and his speed, added to the 80 mph of the enemy plane, added up to 160 mph. Since shooting 60 mph ducks with a shotgun was considered tricky, he could well see that shooting planes with a pistol might be impossible at 160 mph.

What remained with him was the stability of his target as seen through the blades of his propeller. It was a tantalizing vision. At 1,200 rpms the twin-bladed propeller whirled by so fast it was all but invisible, and he became obsessed with the idea that what he could see through he could shoot through. Several times in the next few days he played a dangerous game of his own, flying directly toward German observation planes while he drew a bead on them through imaginary sights on his cowling. The results were better even than he had anticipated. With a little delicate work on the stick and rudder pedals, he found he could aim his entire aircraft with more ease and accuracy than he could swing a shotgun.

Now that he had discovered his airplane to have the aiming characteristics of a perfect weapon, he was more frustrated than ever. Cold facts told him that each blade passed before his eyes 20 times a second—40 wide, wooden blades every time he counted, "One." To fire a single shot through that invisible circle meant that in one second—one inhaled breath—he had 40 chances of blasting off his own prop. Even for the wild Garros the odds looked discouraging. Especially when it wasn't a pistol or a rifle he wanted to fire. He wanted to fire a machine gun at ten rounds per second. Take ten bullets and 40 propeller blades and march them past a given point in a second and you had shingles going through a buzz saw.

He voiced his frustrations at the escadrille's nightly sessions of hangar flying in the local Buc gin mill, and got some attention. The idea that a pilot could sight his plane with the same accuracy that an infantryman could sight his rifle was new and enticing. In the next few weeks the idea spread through both the British and French flying forces, and sev-

The machine gun in this post-WW I display is the Hotchkiss 303, the same type used by Roland Garros. It was a small, light automatic that fired a clip of 25 bullets in approximately five seconds.

Jarrett WW I Museum

eral efforts were made to circumvent the propeller. One British idea was to mount a machine gun on a tripod above the pilot. This put its bullets above the tips of the propeller blades, but it had the unfortunate handicap of putting the gun itself above the reach of the pilot. At best it could fire its 25-round clip in three seconds, not to be reloaded again on that mission. At worst, if it misfired and needed a swat or two to start it up, as it frequently did, it was beyond reach.

The next effort, made by both the British and French, was to mount the machine guns out on the wings beyond the arc of the propeller. This had all the disadvantages of the tripod mount, plus some others that were more fatal. If the recoil didn't knock the wings off with the first burst, it was almost certain to weaken the wing roots and unseat a few flying wires. And then there was the effort to fire through a hollow crankshaft in the engine. This brought the recoil back between the pilot's legs, and if that wasn't unnerving enough, it so filled the cockpit with powder smoke that the pilot was either blinded or choked out of action.

Naturally these unfriendly efforts did not escape the attention of the Germans. They began equipping their two-place observation planes with machine guns mounted on a swivel. The casual, friendly salute gave way to a burst of machine gun fire as the observer manned his gun to cover both sides and the rear. Still there was no real danger. The machine guns were purely defensive gestures, and all one had to do was not approach German planes. Attack was out of the question. Not with machine guns that could only fight a rear-guard action.

One of the really amazing facts of World War I is that amidst all the struggles to arm airplanes with lethal weapons the method of synchronizing a gun to fire through a propeller had already been found. On July 15, 1913, Franz Schneider, a German, patented a practical synchronizing system. Two brothers in England had also designed a usable synchronizing system only to have their plans pigeonholed by the war office. Even a Russian came up with a simple mechanism for firing a gun through a propeller.

Reported to be the first plane built with a synchronized gun for the pilot was an L.V.G. two-seater monoplane created by Franz Schneider. The design was not ordered into production, however.

Then, on February 8, 1915, Armand Pinsard, the man acclaimed by Garros as, "The best friend I ever had," conked out over German-occupied territory. With that strange sense of gallantry that still persisted among airmen, the next day a German pilot dropped a note over the airfield at Buc announcing that Armand was alive and in good hands for the duration of the war. According to the cheerful tenor of the note, that meant he would be held in durance vile for about six weeks. The normally wild Garros at that moment lost his last slipping hold on what common sense he had left.

The day after Pinsard went down, Garros stalked into a shed occupied by the maintenance representative of the Hotchkiss machine gun company. The Hotchkiss was a small, light automatic that fired a clip of 25 bullets in five seconds. With a good man shoving in fresh clips, it could deliver about 200 high-velocity, long-range bullets a minute without overheating. Garros had an idea.

"I want to mount a Hotchkiss on my cowling aimed exactly on my line of flight," he said grimly. "I have it figured out. If I fire a clip of twenty-five, I will get eighteen between the propeller blades. . . ."

"And the other seven will chop off your propeller."

"I am not concerned about that. I will come down, yes, but I will glide in unharmed. The German plane, too, will come down under conditions not so satisfactory. As long as I remain over French territory, no Germans can fly over to spy on us."

"But the risk! You shoot off your own propeller to bring down a German plane, and maybe—"

"So what does a propeller cost compared to a German plane and crew? Fix me up. The Germans hold my friend. I want to bring down Germans."

The expert didn't have to give the problem much thought. The previous year R. Saulnier of the Morane-Saulnier aircraft firm had borrowed a Hotchkiss gun from the French government and experimented with a synchronizing gear system. Some of the bullets had "hung fire" and ripped into the propeller. So Saulnier had fixed steel plates to the prop in order to deflect the bullets. But when the war had burst upon the scene, Saulnier had to return the gun and the idea was temporarily placed in the back of his mind.

The three men, the representative from Hotchkiss, Garros and Saulnier, got together.

When Garros returned to Escadrille M.S. 23 in March he flew a Morane-Saulnier N. Mounted on the fuselage was a fixed forward-firing Hotchkiss machine gun. Saulnier bullet-deflectors protected the propeller.

Most records agree that it was on April 1 when four German two-place Albatros observation planes armed with machine guns in the rear came over the French lines just north of Paris. Up to meet them came a tiny Morane-Saulnier monoplane powered with a Le Rhône rotary motor. It was to laugh. Maybe it still is, but it worked. The Le Rhône required that the propeller be attached to the motor itself instead of the crankshaft. In action, the crankshaft remained rigidly stationary while the motor spun around it. Yet it produced in the Morane a flying speed of 80 mph.

It was a clear day, and thousands of troops in trenches on both sides of the shambles called No Man's Land watched with awe the events that followed.

Garros was at the controls, and he was a man whose seething months of frustration were about to burst. He headed into the first plane so fast and furiously that he was barely able to zoom over the aerial debris after firing his first round.

The pilots and observer-gunners of the remaining three planes couldn't grasp what had happened. The reports of the survivors mention that they saw the flames of machine gun fire "between the blades of the propeller," but knowing this was impossible, they thought the Morane had knocked the wings off their Albatros with its undercarriage. Indeed, Garros' pass was close enough to the doomed Albatros to create that illusion, and when he

German Imperial Air Force

THE MAN WHO PUT WINGS ON WAR

went into his falling-leaf act with a tail-spin finale, the illusion was perfect.

The three planes circled above their falling comrade in bewilderment, hoping to the last moment to see the Albatros straighten out and land safely. It plowed in, nose first, and exploded.

By that time Garros had regained his altitude. Once more flames sparkled brightly between the blades of his propeller. This time the bullets of his second clip raked through gas tanks and motor, and the second Albatros exploded in mid-air.

Garros dived, his piano-wire rigging screaming. With two remaining machine gunners alerted, the safest place was underneath. It was a needless maneuver. With two of their planes converted into fire balls in three minutes, the surviving pilots were heading for home at full throttle.

Garros did not follow. He had a weapon designed to meet the Germans head-on, and he saw no reason to fly into machine gun bullets designed for rear-guard action. He turned his Morane back to his landing field, super-elated at scoring a double, and completely oblivious to the fact that his propeller had been knocked askew and was setting up a fearful vibration. It was working, wasn't it?

For the sake of the record, the first two men shot down in aerial combat were Sub-Lieutenant Hugo Ackner and Observer-Gunner Fritz Dietrichs. With their deaths, air combat would never be the same.

It was a crude, semisuicidal weapon Garros was using. His gun was mounted conveniently in front of him, and by raising up and straddling his stick, he could shove in a fresh clip without too much danger of being pitched out in a nose dive. But every time he pulled the cord that fired a clip, one out of four bullets was slamming into the deflective armor on his propeller blades. He wasn't shooting them off, but he wasn't doing them any good either, nor was he doing much for the alignment of a crankshaft around which a motor spun furiously. Things were going on inside he couldn't appreciate.

The Fokker gun: Anthony Fokker developed the synchronizing mechanism shown above in record time after examining Garros' deflector plates. Fokker was a brilliant inventor; Garros was not. His device was far more sophisticated and gave the Germans a big lead in armament. This is a Parabellum installed in an Eindecker.

Anthony Fokker in his 1915 monoplane (left). Because this early Fokker ship was so similar to the Morane flown by Roland Garros, Fokker was called in to examine the Garros deflector plates. He was then ordered by the German military brass to quickly produce a similar device, but came up with his superior gun synchronizing mechanism.

13

ROLAND GARROS

By April 16 Garros had driven the German planes from the skies above France. To make more kills he had to hunt far behind the German lines, and even then the sight of his little plane was enough to send the pilots fleeing. He knew better than to attack from the rear, but with all opposition fleeing in front of him, it was the only way he could attack. Down he went on four planes and all four gunners, in tight formation, opened up on him.

Fabric was shot from his wings in spurts. His gas tank was riddled, and the fumes of gas spray nearly smothered him. A slug hit his machine gun and fell into his lap. Down he came, picking the leader in order to put the other three gunners behind him.

He saw the pilot stand up in the cockpit to shoot at him with a pistol. "I had to laugh," he said later. Then he pulled the cord, and poured his clip right through man and machine. His only momentary worry was that his own gunfire would ignite the gas leaking all around him.

Garros continued his dive, passing the stricken Aviatik, and then rolled out safely below the other three planes. He headed for home, patting the side of his plane and murmuring words of encouragement. Over No Man's Land he was just above tree-top level and picked up a dozen more rifle bullets from the Germans in the trenches. One of them cut short the few minutes of gas he had left, and he went in just behind the French lines. It wouldn't be Garros if he didn't pull his crash in full view of an assortment of generals making an inspection tour of the front, and that night, wearing only a black eye for his crack-up, he was decorated with the *Legion d'Honneur*.

The newspapers, hungry for any kind of a victory, ran his story throughout the Allied world. Five planes in 16 days. In hunting for words to describe his glory, one reporter enthused, "With five planes to his credit, he is an ace among pilots," and thus began the legend that it takes five planes to make an ace.

Three days later, on April 19, Garros went hunting again behind the German lines. He felt some vibration from his motor, but by this time he would have felt strange in a plane that didn't vibrate. Over the railroad yards at Courtrai he tossed out a couple of bombs

Smithsonian Institution

Three machine guns firing through the propeller (left) was Anthony Fokker's ultimate development of the crude Garros idea. The installation was made on a Fokker E-4 which was flown briefly by Immelmann, but had to be discarded because the three guns were too heavy.

Anthony Fokker was later called upon to produce synchronizing mechanisms for planes of other makes. Here (right) he is explaining his installation on an Albatros D-1 to a group of pilots of *Jasta 2*. In background, second from the right, is the great Oswald Boelcke, then the commander of the *Jasta*.

he had been carrying in his lap, and was disappointed when no ammunition train blew up on the siding. He started his turn for home, and it was then that the vibration increased to a dreadful shaking. He eased back on the throttle, but his motor was beyond tender care. Near Ingelmunster, 40 miles from the Dutch frontier, he saw a clearing in a forest and went in. Thinking he was alone in the wilderness, he climbed out leisurely, and according to custom, tried to set fire to his plane. The damn thing wouldn't burn. He was still lighting matches when the woods came alive with German soldiers, and he became a guest of the Kaiser.

That was at 8:00 a.m. By noon his plane had been identified as the one that had chased the German planes out of the sky. By 5:00 p.m., contrary to all military procedure, red tape was cast aside and Garros and his plane were on their way to Berlin.

For Garros, it was his last visit all over again. Many German fliers were there to toast a gallant birdman with champagne, and Garros was gallant enough to play the piano, that being the custom in those days. But this time when he pleaded his teeth were afloat, a guard went with him, and when at last he went to bed that night, it was in the jug.

His plane, meanwhile, had been given a thorough inspection, with special attention to the bullet-deflecting collar. Anthony Fokker was brought in with urgent instructions to prepare similar collars for the German planes.

The great airplane designer studied the bullet-scarred collars for less than ten seconds. "They won't work," he said flatly.

"But they do work," he was informed just as flatly.

"Luck," he said.

"Luck or no luck, we must have them. Within a week. Get busy." According to Fokker's own letters on the subject, his instructions were even briefer than that, and colored with profane language.

Garros had proved that machine gun bullets could be fired through the propeller blades, and had thus established a fact. Fokker could not deny the fact, but he still could dislike the method. As a great designer, which Garros was not, he could see that the constant hammering of bullets against a collar would sooner or later, and usually sooner, wreck an

Smithsonian Institution

airplane. He marveled both aloud and in his own writings that Garros had survived the first burst. (In this line of thought he was quite right. After the capture of Garros, both the French and English tried to use his collar and in all instances their pilots shot off their propellers or were forced to land when excessive vibration threatened to tear off their wings or motors.)

Fokker had one idea based on an unusual experiment in his youth. He was a Hollander, and one day in his boyhood he had tried throwing stones through the vanes of a windmill. Only half of his rocks got through until he discovered that if he threw just as a vane swung past the vertical, he could get through every time. Now it was a matter of getting bullets through before a propeller blade could intercept them. In a flash he had the idea of letting the blade itself trigger the gun. Twenty-four sleepless hours later he had worked out the timing to get his triggering from the crankshaft. Through a push-pull rod geared to the crankshaft, the trigger would be activated during those intervals when the blades were not in the line of fire and then released during that split second when the blade was passing the muzzle. Forty-eight sleepless hours later he had it working on the ground, and 72 sleepless hours later, he had it working in the air.

In one of the greatest production speed records in the history of warfare, less than a month after the capture of Garros, the famed German pilot, Oswald Boelcke, brought down his first French plane using a machine gun synchronized with his propeller. Now it was the Germans who cleared the skies of Allied planes.

If Garros' career was at a standstill, it was not the end. His second escape from the Germans was quite as sensational as the first. True, his old friend Armand Pinsard helped in this exploit with a few well-placed bribes, but that in no way discounts the fact that on the pitch-black night of January 23, 1918, Sergeant John Quette flew an old Horace Farman biplane into a rocky pasture outside Cologne while overhead Pinsard flew cover in a Spad. Nor does it discount the fact that Quette and his passenger boosted the Farman out of the pasture, and that by dawn Quette, Pinsard and Garros were well into a bottle of cognac with several more bottles standing by in reserve.

Back in the air again, Garros found himself up against the hard law of averages he had introduced when he put wings on death. Three weeks was the average life of a pilot. He did better. From February to October he roamed the skies.

Then on the morning of October 5, a month before the end of the war, a German Fokker D-7 slid down out of the sun, and Roland Garros never knew what hit him. A knight of the air, yes, but with a difference he himself had introduced. When the knights of old were unhorsed, they got up and walked away. The knights of the air never did. •

Eugene Gilbert (left) was a fellow pilot of Garros in Escadrille M.S. 23 and worked with him in his front-fire experiments. He is one of the few pilots of record to take the deflection plates into action, and some historians have credited him with originating the idea of a deflector on the propeller. A prewar pilot as Garros was, Gilbert spent a year as a prisoner of war and was killed in a test flight accident after his escape and later return to France.

Les Archives d'Art et d'Histoire Photographique, Paris

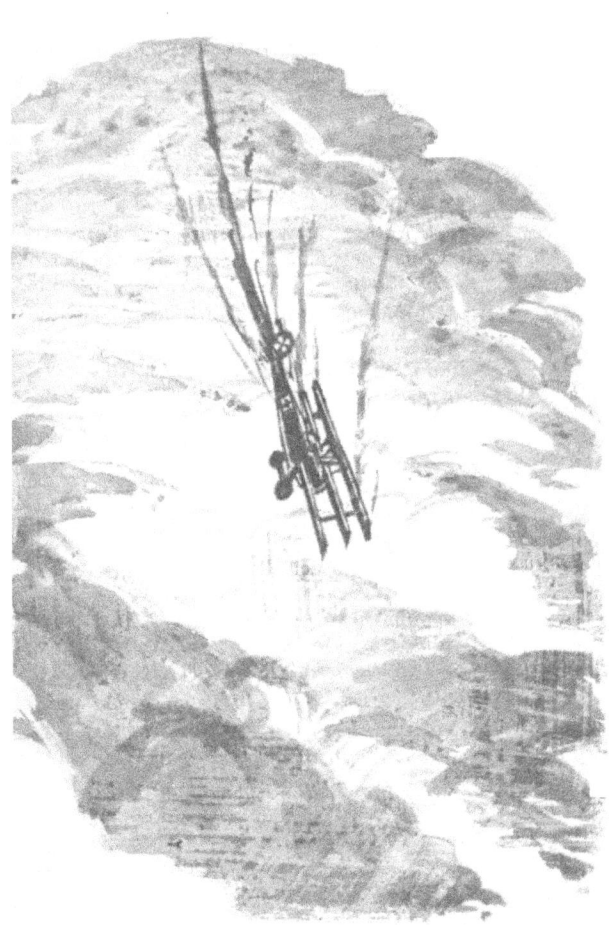

Werner Voss
Pride of the Hussars

By William E. Barrett

WERNER VOSS at 17 was a dark-haired, blue-eyed German boy, only medium-tall but straight and strong. He wore the uniform of the Krefeld Hussars, a very swank uniform with heavy braiding on a dark blue jacket, a dolman hanging from the left shoulder, a busby on his head. He wore the uniform only two nights a week, of course, and for two months in summer because the Krefeld Hussars were a militia company; but at 17 a boy likes to swagger in a colorful uniform and not everyone could qualify for the cavalry.

The Voss family was an old family in Krefeld, a city renowned for its production of velvets and silks and its fine technical schools. Werner, the eldest son, planned to follow the ancient craft of his father, a dyer, who was possessed of the secrets which had made German dyes superior to any in the world. At 17, however, he was still a student. His father regarded his pride in the hussar uniform with amused tolerance. The older man had in his own youth, like all other healthy Germans, played at being a soldier but he had never been to war. He did not expect his son to experience war. Germany remained at peace because Germany was strong. There had been no war since 1870, some 44 years. Only very old people remembered the last one.

Werner Voss rode to summer maneuvers three days after his seventeenth birthday and the adventure, of course, was not "play."

The militia company was commanded by former officers of the regular army and German discipline was iron hard and unbending. Werner rode and took his horse over jumps, he engaged in precise mounted drill and he participated in the most thrilling of all German cavalry exercises, the grand charge, in which the hussars rode knee to knee. He also took care of his horse and equipment, did his share of sentry duty and learned to live in the open without barrack comforts.

On June 28, 1914 a Serbian fanatic assassinated the Archduke Franz Ferdinand, heir to the Austrian throne, and his Duchess in the streets of Sarajevo. The news was late in reaching the encampment of the Krefeld Hussars and it produced no excitement. The event was shocking but it was remote. It did not remain remote for long. Within a month Austria-Hungary declared war on Serbia, Russia went to the assistance of the Serbs in defiance of a German warning and the torch that was to set a world on fire was ablaze. Young Germans were no longer playing soldier or just putting in their required military service; overnight they *were* soldiers.

On the first of August came the German declaration of war on Russia and the Krefeld Hussars received orders to move. It was an exciting time for young men and the hussars were disappointed when they learned that they were not heading for the Russian frontier. Their orders took them to the French border of Lorraine. While they were enroute France and Germany declared war upon each other. The French launched the attack in Lorraine and poured into Germany driving the border garrisons before them. To the north Germany sent her mighty army through Belgium to flank the French fortifications and, on the fourth of August, England declared war on Germany.

Werner Voss was in action on August 28 when the Germans launched a drive that forced the French back across the border. It was open warfare in Lorraine and the cavalry, as they were intended to be, were the eyes of the army. They rode in advance of the infantry and scouted the terrain and they fought French cavalry units engaged in the same work. No one on either side realized that this battle in Lorraine was to be the last in the long history of the world in which cavalry was to play a vital role. Already in the north cavalry was dismounted as the war developed into a struggle of huge infantry masses. Werner Voss was helping to make history and did not know it.

Other German youths serving on the many German fronts were destined, as Voss was, to serve ultimately in the cavalry of the sky

Werner Voss, one of Germany's greatest aces and a contemporary and rival of Baron Manfred von Richthofen, is shown here in a relaxed moment. His achievements have been passed over by many authors despite the fact that he scored 48 confirmed victories and was awarded the *Pour le Mérite* for valor.

The Aviatik C-2 (right) was the first ship Werner Voss piloted in action, a slow and cumbersome observation ship of 1915. The pilot sat in the rear cockpit without a gun while the bomber-gunner in the front cockpit had two.

which was to take over the functions of the hussars. Baron von Richthofen was one. A graduate of the military school and a second lieutenant of the First Uhlans, he rode into Russia with the first attack then transferred to Belgium when the slowing German drive required reinforcements. Lothar von Richthofen, his brother, was with a dragoon regiment on the Marne. Bruno Loerzer, lieutenant in a provincial infantry regiment, was at Baden. Ernst Udet was riding a motorcycle as a courier in Alsace. Hermann Goering, also in Alsace, was wounded in the first engagement and taken to a hospital. Werner Voss knew nothing about any of them and had no interest in airplanes.

The excitement in Lorraine did not last long. By October the French and Germans settled down to holding operations with the winter coming on. The big battles were in the north and Lorraine became relatively unimportant although men died there. When it became apparent during the winter that the hussars had no future in this war save as foot soldiers, Werner Voss turned his eyes to the air. The flying service was new, it called for the qualities of a good cavalryman and no man who has ever ridden to war is content to march. Werner Voss was an *unteroffizier*, the lowest noncom rank but one that he could not have hoped to achieve before 19 during peacetime. He wore the Iron Cross which he had earned through gallantry in action. He applied for pilot training in the German Imperial Air Force.

It was August 1915 before he was accepted and by then he was a veteran, 18 years old, the holder of the Iron Cross of the First Class, unwounded after a year of war. Other cavalrymen were ahead of him. Manfred von Richthofen was flying as an observer on the Russian front and had already been shot down once before Werner Voss reported at the flying school. The careers of these two men were destined to cross and recross many times, but in the beginning von Richthofen's advantage was very great. He was a member of the officer caste and although he failed to qualify as a pilot in training, he took his commission into the air as an observer before the humble son of a dyer, a lowly noncom, started at the foot of the ladder.

Werner Voss was a natural pilot whereas Manfred von Richthofen was not. Voss took to an airplane as he took to a horse; with sure judgment and a steady hand on the controls. He won his wings in record time and his aptitude earned him an assignment that he did not want. He became an instructor in the flying school. There was an increasing demand for pilots and a need for good pilot instructors. A man like Voss with decorations

Richard Hardin

WERNER VOSS

and a year of service at the front added authority and prestige to the staff even if he was only 18.

The war in the air, Werner felt, had passed him by. German flyers like Boelcke and Immelmann were making great reputations, bombing squadrons were attacking enemy installations, observation planes were doing the work of cavalry, Zeppelins were attacking England. He was missing all of that, but he did his job during the winter and into the spring of the new year, 1916, when aerial activity became intense. He trained men to fly and congratulated them when they got their orders to go to the front, the orders that he envied.

In May 1916, unexpectedly, his orders came. The newly organized *Kampgeschwader No. 1* needed the pick of German pilots even if instructors had to be taken from the schools. A group of six flights, it was charged with the double duty of bombing and fighting on the Somme front where the British were massing men and munitions for a big push. Werner Voss was jubilant.

"I am a soldier again and not a professor," he wrote home. "When we have smashed the British, the war will be over. I am happy that I will have a part in it."

He had no thought of danger or death, only of victory and glory. He was given a new Aviatik two-seater and he was delighted with it. It was slow and tiring to fly although the streamlining was better than an earlier model. There was one unique feature. The pilot sat in the rear cockpit without a gun while the bomber-gunner in the front cockpit had two guns, one on a tripod that fired to the rear over the pilot's head and one mounted on an angle so that it fired past the edge of the propeller arc. For some reason the Germans had been unable to fit a synchronized machine gun to the Benz engine which powered the ship.

Werner Voss flew and fought through the long battle of the Somme in this ship and the dream of glory died early. The British with their pushers—the Vickers Gunbus, the D. H. 2 and the F. E.—and the Nieuport scouts which they had purchased from the French, had command of the air. Individual British aces like Ball and Hawker were so well known that desperate Germans had learned to recognize them in the air. Two-seaters were cold meat and it was a joke to call the Aviatik a fighter.

On his nineteenth birthday Werner Voss was promoted to flight leader but there was little glory in that. He was still a noncom and the occasion of his promotion saw a British victory. On that day the squadron was all but annihilated. He was the only pilot left who had flown to the Somme a month earlier with the exception of Baron von Gerstoff, the commander. On June 17 Werner Voss saw von Gerstoff shot down in flames over the Ancre. That same day Boelcke, the great chaser pilot, was also shot down. It was believed for a time that he, too, had been

German Imperial Air Force

Young veteran Voss who started the war in 1914 as a cavalryman, became a flying instructor in 1915 at the age of 18, transferred to an aerial observation squadron in May 1916 and later developed into one of the great fighting aces of the war. He died in the air Sept. 23, 1917.

killed but he landed his badly shattered ship safely behind his own lines. The equally famous ace Count Max Immelmann was not so fortunate. On June 18 he was killed in combat.

The events of those two days sank the morale of the German Imperial Air Force to a new low. In the mess of *Kampgeschwader No. 1* men grumbled and swore. They were supposed to be a bombing squadron and they did not even have the satisfaction of seeing their bombs go down on the enemy. The British attacked and routed them in their own air space before they could cross the lines. Voss listened to them. He had his own thoughts and his own memories. He was the only one in the room who had known every man on the long casualty list of the squadron, the originals and the replacements. Many of them had been his pupils before they were his comrades.

"The Englischer who defeats me must kill me in the air," he said. "I will not surrender to him on the ground."

He stopped the griping with a single statement but he knew that the griping was justified. He had been fortunate, but he did not expect to survive the odds forever. He lived as the others did: from one patrol to the next.

On July 4 he was given a reprieve. The schools and the factories of Germany sent new men and machines to the Somme front and the old embattled squadrons were withdrawn. Werner Voss went home on leave to Krefeld where he had played at being a soldier just two years ago. Now, in spite of his youth, he was no longer a boy.

During that summer of 1916 the German Imperial Air Force was redesigned and rebuilt. Oswald Boelcke was given the task of organizing the chaser scouts into two compact fighting units made up of the best pilots in the German service. His own *Jasta*, *Jagdstaffel 2*, was composed of men he had personally selected and included Baron Manfred von Richthofen who had been flying two-seaters in Russia after experience as both observer and pilot on the Verdun front. Given his pick of the new chaser planes available, Boelcke selected the Albatros D-1. The other chaser, the Halberstadt scout, was assigned to *Jagdstaffel 3* which was to be manned by other carefully selected pilots.

Werner Voss was assigned to *Jasta 3* after training on the Halberstadt at Grossenhain in Saxony. He bore a brand new commission as second lieutenant dated September 1, but did not go into action until the end of October when *Jagdstaffel 2* was already famous. Every man in the Boelcke Squadron had scored victories and Manfred von Richthofen had six.

On the day that Werner Voss flew his first patrol, Boelcke was killed in a collision with one of his own men.

The weather was bad and with winter inactivity settling over the battle front there were few British planes in the sky, but on November 19 Voss scored his first victory by shooting down a British B.E. 2b behind German lines. He was elated and yet depressed.

"The poor devils!" he wrote in a letter home, "I know how they felt. I have flown in such a ship. They must be destroyed because they spy out our secrets but I would prefer to shoot down the chasers."

He shot down one of "the chasers" on the following day, the first of many. He was to become unique among the aces, one of the few—if not the only one—who numbered more fighting scouts than two-seaters on his tally sheet.

On November 20, 1916 Werner Voss scored his second victory and Baron Manfred von Richthofen scored his ninth and tenth. The German propaganda machine was already planning to capitalize on the wonderful asset that was theirs; a titled member of the military caste who was the ideal successor to Boelcke and more than that; the man who, with good fortune, would make the people forget Boelcke. He would need the good fortune. *Jagdstaffel 2* after its amazing success in the first few weeks of operation had suffered heavily at the hands of the British. When *Oberleutnant* Stephen Kirmaier took command of *Jagdstaffel 2* on October 30 there were only three pilots surviving out of Boelcke's original 14. He lasted only three weeks himself before he was shot down on November 22. When Captain Walz succeeded him on November 29 there were two vacancies in *Jasta 2*. Werner Voss was requisitioned to fill one of them.

Werner Voss forgot that he was a battle-scarred veteran when he received the news of his transfer. He acted like the boy of 19 that

WERNER VOSS

he actually was. He drank too much beer and drank toasts to the comrades he was leaving without giving a thought to the fact that his jubilation was anything but a compliment to *Jasta 3*. His happy binge was in celebration of what he considered a promotion; a transfer to the *Jasta* that bore the famous name of "Boelcke," a transfer that made him the comrade of von Richthofen, of Schaefer, of Allmenroeder. *Hoch!*

It was December, a bad flying month, when Voss joined *Jagdstaffel 2*. He was awed at meeting the great Manfred von Richthofen to whose flight he was assigned. The Baron had just won his most famous victory in a duel with Major Lanoe Hawker, England's leading ace, and his score was 11 victories. He was short, shorter than Voss and slender, fair haired with level searching eyes and a friendly smile. The smile however was reserved for trusted comrades and for first greetings. He was a firm disciplinarian with young pilots and he did not fraternize with them in the mess.

Werner Voss flew at Richthofen's right on his first two patrols. The ships of Boelcke *Jasta* like those of *Jasta 3* were painted in various dull colors and combinations of colors which represented mainly an attempt at camouflage. Richthofen as a gesture of defiance or disdain had his Albatros painted a bright red. There were no British in the air and those first patrols were dull, but in spite of this the Baron lectured Voss for what he described as "a lack of alertness" on the first patrol and for not maintaining close formation on the second. Werner's request for permission to fly a solo patrol was turned down as "unthinkable," although he had flown many such patrols in *Jasta 3* and had downed his Nieuport on one of them. It was all part of the discipline which Baron von Richthofen considered necessary in any flight that he led. After those first two patrols he selected Voss as top man. He was to stay above the flight whenever it was attacked and to come down to the rescue if any member of the flight got into trouble.

The assignment was a compliment and a vote of confidence, but Voss did not realize this. He believed that the Baron had a poor opinion of him and he disliked the watchdog role which sidelined him during an attack. From his vantage point aloft, Voss watched Richthofen score four victories in December and bring his total to 15. Werner Voss did not score any victories and his total remained at two. He began to doubt that he belonged in *Jagdstaffel* Boelcke.

The German War office had completed its plans for Manfred von Richthofen by the first of January. As a propaganda asset and a superb air fighter he could not be left in the *Jagdstaffel* that bore the name of another German airman. With much publicity fanfare he was given a *Jagdstaffel* of his own, No. 11, and permitted to take with him his pick of the Boelcke *Jasta*. He selected Schaefer and Allmenroeder, the two men who had survived with him since *Jasta 2's* first day on the front.

Voss and the other young pilots of the Boelcke *Jagdstaffel* drew long breaths of relief when the three veterans departed on January 15. So, too, did Captain Walz, the com-

Wide World

Baron Manfred von Richthofen, the top ranking ace of WW I. His only serious rival was Voss, who lacked the propaganda backing given Richthofen and who was not a member of the officer caste. Werner Voss, however, was a natural pilot; Manfred von Richthofen was not.

mander, who favored personal initiative over rigid discipline in aerial warfare. To celebrate the *Jasta* scored three victories on its first patrol after the departure of Richthofen. Voss scored one of those victories and the following day he scored another on a solo patrol, shooting down a D.H. 2, out of a flight of five, that he surprised within sight of the German antiaircraft gunners. Bernert, one of Voss' best friends who had never been outstanding while the Baron was with the *Jasta*, shot down five British planes in one day.

In the meantime the pilots of Boelcke *Jasta* watched the new *Jasta 11* with professional interest. Von Richthofen's first act, either his own idea or an inspiration from the propaganda office, was to adopt the color red as the distinctive marking of his *Jasta*. His own Albatros was painted a solid red. Schaefer's was red and black, Allmenroeder's red and white, Lothar von Richthofen's red and yellow. The other pilots worked out various combinations but red predominated in all of them.

"We, too, need plumage," Voss said.

Boelcke *Jasta* had never had distinctive individual markings on planes but Werner Voss received permission from the amiable Walz to paint his ship and the other pilots followed his example. The Voss D-1 Albatros was decorated in black and white squares, a checkerboard design, and as an added inspiration had the skull insigne of The Death's-Head Hussars painted on the side of the fuselage. The hussars no longer rode but Werner Voss took their once feared insigne into the air. He scored two victories in one day to baptize that insigne and to introduce his checkerboard to the front.

His score mounted fast despite the bad weather. Between January 15 and February 15 he destroyed ten British planes, seven scouts and three two-seaters, bringing his total to 12. Manfred von Richthofen in the same period, flying the new Albatros D-3, one of the greatest ships of the war, downed four two-seaters and one scout bringing his score to 20.

Werner Voss was still very much in awe of the Baron and had no thought of personal rivalry—not yet.

He was confident of his own skill, however, and continued to hunt alone in addition to his regular circus patrols. In this he resembled the British aces Ball and McCudden and the French ace Guynemer; the only German pilot of his time who did.

The checkerboard plane was a familiar

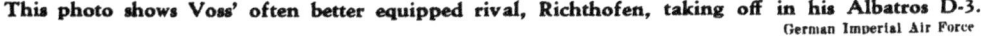

This photo shows Voss' often better equipped rival, Richthofen, taking off in his Albatros D-3.
German Imperial Air Force

sight over the British lines and its activities were noted in many British diaries by airmen who did not know the pilot's name. It flew out of nowhere, surprising English flyers who never expected the Germans to hunt except in packs. The checkerboard pilot never hesitated to attack flights of five or seven planes, shooting down one out of the flight and zooming away before the others could engage him.

Voss gloried in these forays and he had perfected a new technique which no one else on either side of the line used. He would come in high so that his selected victim believed that the checkerboard plane would pass over him; then, with split second timing, he would sideslip, pouring bullets into his startled foe while slipping.

By March 23 he had 16 victories and he was cited in the dispatches with a medal for valor. He celebrated that decoration with two victories on March 24. He scored four more victories before March was over and now he was second only to the great Baron in the tally sheet of the German Imperial Air Force. *Jagdstaffel 2,* thanks to Voss, was prominent in the daily dispatches and the name of Boelcke still rivaled that of von Richthofen.

On April 2, 1917 Werner Voss visited Manfred von Richthofen on *Jasta 11's* drome at Douai representing Captain Walz who was ill. It was a critical time on the front and Walz considered close liaison between the two *Jagdstaffels* imperative. The German army had retreated to the Hindenburg line and the British were massing men and munitions for a new assault. The Germans needed observation behind the British lines and they wanted no British observation probing the strength and the weakness of their new positions. The Albatros D-3 was coming out of the factory in quantity, but Voss had only the D-2

This meeting was a contrast to the first between Manfred von Richthofen and Werner Voss. Voss was no awed rookie now. He had 23 victories and the Baron, five years older than he was and many months longer on the front, had 32. Von Richthofen was friendly and affable, a good host with none of the cold reserve that he had manifested when they served together in the same *Jasta.*

"You have been doing well," he said. "I hear great things of you. Tell me, how do you do it?"

Voss smiled. "I fly and I shoot. What can I tell *you* about fighting?"

Under the Baron's friendliness, Voss sensed something else. There was no meanness in Manfred von Richthofen, no trickiness, nor lack of generosity,. but there had

R. R. Martin

always been a broad streak of jealousy in him. He had been jealous of his brother Lothar when they were boys because Lothar was taller, and he had been jealous again when Lothar's dragoon regiment had a better chance of distinguishing itself in the first weeks of the war than had the First Uhlans. He liked to excel, to be first in everything. He became savagely impatient with anybody or anything which came between him and his objectives. Since the death of Boelcke he had been the one great name in the German Imperial Air Force and the other publicized names had been associated with his, members of the *Jagdstaffel* flying in his shadow. The rise of this upstart, Voss, a mere reserve officer in a de-emphasized *Jasta* which he himself had looted of its best men, bewildered him. He was friendly because he appreciated flying and fighting skill, because Voss served brilliantly the same ends that he served; but he did not like the thought that the ace who was second on the victory roster was not one of his men.

Manfred von Richthofen returned again and again to the subject of Voss' victories as they talked together, and the younger man became thoughtful. He had dreamed of equaling or surpassing the Red Baron but he did not expect that to happen. Until this day he had remained too much in awe of Manfred von Richthofen to consider himself seriously as a rival. When he gained the impression from Richthofen's attitude that the Baron considered *him* a rival, all of his thinking changed.

"Come, I will fly home with you," Richthofen said when the interview was over. "It is not good to fly alone."

Voss, who flew often alone and not behind his own lines, was amused. "It is a bad day," he said, "and who will fly with you when you return?"

"Lothar will accompany us."

They were joined by Lothar von Richthofen, summoned by his brother, as they walked out to their ships. It was indeed a bad day, cold and windy with intermittent snow. The ships took off with Manfred von Richthofen leading. It was an interesting flight even if it was only planned as a short trip behind the German lines between two dromes: two von Richthofens and Werner Voss.

The three machines climbed to between 12,000 and 14,000 feet in order to clear two levels of cloud. The Baron flew a long arc toward the front lines, not approaching them too closely. Voss understood his purpose

Anthony Fokker

The Albatros D-3 (left), one of the great ships of the war. Richthofen scored many of his victories in this ship as did his one foremost rival, Werner Voss.

Anthony Fokker credited Voss with saving his classic triplane —the D.R. 1—from oblivion after Richthofen rejected it. Richthofen was an Albatros man and did not like the triplane, but Voss was immediately taken by its maneuverability. Even the Baron was later won over. Voss is shown (left) with Anthony Fokker and Rheinhold Platz (background), Fokker's chief engineer, probably the designer of the D.R. 1 and believed to be the genius behind Fokker.

and approved. There was no point in spending the time of three pilots and the fuel of three machines on a mere journey if the trip could be made profitable. The British need for reports on German forces was actually so urgent at that period of the Somme that their old two-seaters flew in all weather and penetrated deeply into German air.

Halfway to the drome of Boelcke *Jasta* they saw six British two-seaters, Sopwith one-and-a-half Strutters, below them scurrying toward home already possessed, no doubt, of the information that they had flown to obtain. The Baron peeled off and went down like a red arrow. The Albatros D-3, beautifully streamlined and powered with the 200 horsepower Mercedes, was the fastest ship on the front and phenomenal in a dive. Lothar followed his brother. Werner Voss in his Albatros D-2, some 30 horsepower less and inferior in streamlining, could not keep up with them.

Voss saw the red Albatros overtake the rearmost Sopwith, firing on it from the perfect above-and-behind attack position. Lothar's plane hurdled his brother's and went after the others. One of the Sopwiths, probably the flight leader trying to protect his flock, banked about to come to the rescue of the attacked plane but when the pilot saw Lothar and Voss above him, he dived away toward the clouds.

The action was incredibly fast as it always was in aerial battles. Voss, resigned to the fact that he had no chance of catching the Sopwiths, leveled off above the Baron and his foe. One did not interfere with Manfred von Richthofen when he had the advantage in a combat. To come to his assistance would imply that he needed assistance and he would never forgive that. Voss merely watched.

The rear gun of the Sopwith was silent and there was no sign of a gunner so Voss assumed that the Baron had killed the gunner with the first burst. The Sopwith pilot was maneuvering desperately, chasing tails with the faster ship which was built less for dogfighting than for swift, annihilating attack. Richthofen fired and missed, fired and missed again. The one-and-a-half Strutter, although a two-seater, was the first British ship on the front with a synchronized gun permitting front fire for the pilot and was six weeks ahead of the first scouts to be so equipped. The pilot, however, could not get a shot at his attacker. He broke off combat and dived into a cloud but it was too thin to protect him and the two ships immediately emerged again, Richthofen still chasing. Voss shook his head doubtfully. That Britisher should have been dead the moment he broke off and dived away.

There was almost a gale wind blowing toward Germany and as the Sopwith twisted and maneuvered he was being carried deeper into German territory. The great Baron was fighting like an inexperienced youngster. The chase continued right down to the ground with von Richthofen shooting all of the way, and the Englishman crash-landed his ship.

Lothar had returned from a futile chase and the three airmen watched the German

Werner Voss is in the cockpit in this photograph, ready to take off in his Fokker triplane.

PRIDE OF THE HUSSARS

infantry surround the Sopwith. The pilot climbed out without help, but the gunner was lifted limp from the cockpit. Manfred von Richthofen led his two companions to a landing on the drome of *Jasta 2*. The normally cool, detached, self-disciplined Baron was wildly excited, out of all proportion Voss thought, after such a bad show.

"That was my thirty-third," Richthofen said. "In our own lines! You saw it, Voss. What an Englishman! The gunner never gave up. He fired on me even after he was on the ground."

"If he fired on you from the ground, you would be justified in shooting him on the ground," Voss said thoughtfully.

He had seen no fire from the British ship at any time, in the air or on the ground, merely superb flying. He was fairly certain that the gunner had been killed by the first burst. Still, Manfred von Richthofen was not a liar. In the heat of battle he might have imagined what did not happen or Voss might have failed to see all that did happen.

That night Werner Voss wrote a letter home. "I had an interesting flight today with Baron von Richthofen," he wrote, "and I saw him shoot down a British Sopwith for his thirty-third victory. He is a great fighter and has done wonderful work for the Fatherland, but I do not believe that he is better than I am."

It sounded boastful, perhaps, to his family at home but it was the honestly expressed opinion of a 19-year-old airman who had seen the Red Baron in action that day and who was not impressed, who had lost his awe of a man who was senior to him, who, for the first time, was thinking of himself as a rival of Germany's greatest ace.

As for Manfred von Richthofen, that thirty-third victory of April 2, 1917 was not a typical performance. He was, perhaps, aware

German Imperial Air Force copied by British Imperial War Museum

that Voss was watching him. He might have tried too hard to impress the younger man. Or it might have been an off day.

The weather cleared overnight and Voss flew two morning patrols without coming close to the enemy. His experience with the Baron had made him eager for more victories and he flew alone in the afternoon to one of his great adventures.

The Germans in retreating to the Hindenburg line had flattened, burned and laid waste the miles of territory over which they planned to retreat. This was a true no man's land, a veritable desert over which the British dared not advance until they brought up heavy artillery support. Werner Voss, flying over this expanse alone on April 3, 1917, spotted a lone British B.E., a hapless two-seater rushing home with pictures of the German positions. Voss dived on it and opened fire, attacking from the front and pouring his burst into the engine rather than shooting the observer. He always had a soft spot for two-seater crews.

The B.E. immediately spiraled down into No Man's Land and Voss, flying above it, saw the pilot and observer jump from the plane and run for the British lines which were closer at that point than the German. They did not even wait to set fire to their ship, the customary procedure.

Voss looked around him. There wasn't another ship in the sky. He doubted that he was under observation from the German side of the lines. He had a victory and no possible confirmation. Moreover this was a photography ship and the British might recover it with the pictures that it contained. He made his decision in an instant. Coming around into the wind, he cut his engine and landed beside the ship that he had downed.

He moved very fast then, wrenching the Lewis gun from its mounting in the B.E. rear cockpit, grabbing the plane identification card from the pilot's compartment and releasing the destruction flare which the Englishmen in their haste had forgotten. He was racing back to his own ship when a British patrol, sent out when the two flyers reached the trenches, opened fire on him. The bullets were whistling around him as he climbed into the cockpit and they continued to whistle as he took off but his luck held.

Back on his own drome, he had trophies of his victory—his twenty-third—and bullets in his Albatros that had been fired by infantry. Captain Walz congratulated him on what he called one of the most daring exploits of the war and made a phone report of it to headquarters. It became a much-discussed incident and Baron von Richthofen generously reported it in his own book, *The Red Battleflyer*.

Imperial War Museum

Long identified as Voss (by the author of this article among others), this is actually a photo of *Leutnant* Hartmuth Baldamus, one of the Eindecker pilots with Boelcke and Immelmann. He was credited with 18 victories.

On April 5, Werner Voss received the most crushing blow of his career; an event that left him too dazed and bewildered to be resentful. Boelcke *Jagdstaffel* received orders transferring it to the quiet French front and its place on the all-important British front was taken by a new *Jasta* equipped with the Albatros D-3.

The inside story of those orders has never been told. The only man who might have told it was General von Hoeppner, Commander of the German Imperial Air Force. Von Hoeppner was a former uhlan, a member of the military caste who took command on October 1, 1916. The air force had grown rapidly in size and was badly organized. Von Hoeppner decided that it needed more professional officers with less emphasis upon mere wartime reservists who were not born to military careers. He was responsible for the huge formation policy which deployed airplanes like cavalry and he offered inducements to regular army officers and graduates of the cadet schools to transfer to the air force. He was unable to do anything about Oswald Boelcke who was the biggest name in German aviation in spite of the fact that he was not of the military caste, but he paved the way for the professional soldiers who were developing under Boelcke.

Manfred von Richthofen had only four victories when von Hoeppner took command of the air force, but he had a title, a great name, a great background and he was a former uhlan. Von Hoeppner immediately interested himself in his career and when Boelcke was killed on October 28 the Baron was groomed to be his successor. He received exceptional publicity in the dispatches and by the time he had scored his eighth victory he had every decoration except the *Pour le Mérite,* Germany's highest decoration for valor. Even this award came to Richthofen after his sixteenth victory.

The order of April 5 transferring the Boelcke *Jasta* to the French front was probably in line with the consistent program of pushing the Boelcke name into the past while the von Richthofen name was being built up. The fact that it also removed the son of a dyer, a reserve officer, from the arena where he competed with Germany's great publicity asset might also have been a factor.

At any rate, when Germany's newest fighting single-seaters gave German pilots absolute command of the air on the British front, and when British two-seaters had to fly because the fate of the army depended upon information, Werner Voss in the outmoded Albatros D-2 was transferred with *Jasta 2* to the French front where there was no major battle and no urgent demand upon French pilots to take risks.

During that month of April 1917 Manfred von Richthofen rode Germany's technical superiority over the British to his high point of glory. It was Bloody April and the British lost four planes for every one they brought down (five to one by German count).

The Red Baron destroyed 21 British ships during the month and brought his score to 52. Werner Voss, flying every day and hunting all over the French front on solo patrols, scored only twice. His total was 23, and von Richthofen whom he had dreamed of rivaling seemed hopelessly out of reach. Voss was not even second. Several of "the Baron's gentlemen" passed him on the tally sheet during that month of German dominance. Wolff ended the month with 29 victories, Schaefer with 27 and Lothar von Richthofen, a comparative newcomer with only three victories at the beginning of April, was credited with 20.

Voss had every reason to believe that given the ship that these men flew and their opportunities he would have pressed Manfred von Richthofen for the honors. He shrugged off the lost opportunity.

"That dream is over," he said.

It wasn't over. Not quite. Von Hoeppner recalled Manfred von Richthofen after that great April winning streak and paraded him around Germany to rouse enthusiasm for the air force and to spur recruiting. The Baron was invited to dine with the Kaiser and feted everywhere he went. To keep the name of von Richthofen active on the front during this period, the young Lothar was placed in command of his brother's *Jasta* commanding men older and more experienced than himself. He lasted only one short week before he was shot down, wounded.

The French stepped up their aerial activity in May and Werner Voss shot down eight of them. His score was 34 when Manfred von Richthofen came back from his vacation on June 4.

The days of easy hunting were over for the Baron and his gentlemen. Schaefer and Zeumer, two of his oldest friends, were killed during the week of his return. The British had new fast ships, adequately armed—the S.E. 5, the Camel and the Bristol Fighter —and British pilots were hot for revenge. Von Richthofen did not immediately clash with any of them. He found an old R.E. 8 still flying on June 18 and then scored two mysterious victories on June 23 and 26, unconfirmed, vaguely reported, but credited to him as his fifty-fourth and fifty-fifth. His fifty-sixth and fifty-seventh victories were over ancient R.E. 8s, too. With the new British scouts and fighters all over the sky, neither Richthofen or the other pilots of his *Jasta* turned in any combat reports involving them during the month of June or early July. On July 6 another old ship, an F.E. 2b, shot Manfred von Richthofen down in combat over the Ypres front.

The Red Baron had a near escape from death, a bullet grazing his skull, and he was taken to the hospital in Courtrai. No news release was issued because he was supposed to be invincible, but word spread fast through the air force and it hurt morale. The proud riders of the Albatros were not doing so well now and most of the big winners of April were dead or in the hospital. Of all those actively flying, Werner Voss was once more second in victories, second only to Wolff.

One man who noted that fact, if General von Hoeppner did not, was Anthony Fokker. The designer had gone into eclipse about the same time Voss had. Bloody April was the month of Albatros and Halberstadt, but Fokker now had a new ship—the D.R. 1, a triplane—which he claimed would out-perform anything that the British possessed. Baron von Richthofen had tried it out in June and curtly rejected it as slower than the Albatros, poor in a dive and probably hazardous. None of the other *Jasta* leaders were interested in anything that Richthofen rejected and Fokker was desperate. He talked to Captain Walz, commander of the de-emphasized Boelcke *Jasta*. Walz was retiring because of poor health and Voss was the logical man to succeed him. Fokker talked to Voss.

Werner Voss tried out the new triplane and fell in love with it. It was a pilot's dream ship: not a swift, diving, assault destroyer, but a waltzing boxer that would move in and out, short of wing span (23 feet, 7 inches), and very sensitive to control. Only the top plane had ailerons and the aerofoil casing around the wheel axle was in effect a fourth plane. It was powered by the 110 horsepower Oberursel rotary engine and weighed only 830 pounds. It was capable of climbing to 15,000 feet in 17 minutes.

Werner Voss wanted the triplane and he got it, mainly because the Albatros D-3 pilots were already complaining that the British pursuit ships were too good for them. The front needed new blood, new inspiration, but not the name of Boelcke which belonged to pre-Richthofen history. An order was placed for triplanes. Voss was given a leave and when he returned he was made commander of a new *Jasta* with permission to choose his own pilots from the pool.

Werner Voss had just celebrated his twentieth birthday but he looked like a man of 30 or more. He had been in action almost continuously on the ground and in the air since August 1914. He was lean and hard, but there were lines of tension in his face and his eyes were somber. He could relax and laugh and celebrate, but the occasions were fewer now than they once had been and the responsibilities of command made him, as they had made von Richthofen, a disciplinarian. He had to have men who could be depended upon to do as they were taught to do. Werner Voss had seen too many of the careless die. Recklessness in the proper circumstances he approved, but carelessness, never.

It was mid-August when Voss and his *Jasta 10* reached the Ypres front and found the British in command of the air. On his second day he shot down a Sopwith Camel. One of his flight scored a victory, too, and the Camels, reputedly the best dogfighters of the war, broke off the engagement without inflicting any damage on the "tripes."

That was a beginning. The date was August 20. On the twenty-first Voss shot down an S.E. 5 and on the twenty-second he scored a double victory. He finished the month with a score of 39 and every one of his rookies had at least one victory. He had not lost a man.

There is some dispute among historians on the question of *Jasta 10's* equipment, the dates of the triplane deliveries, and the date of the first Fokker triplane victory which Anthony Fokker once stated was scored by Voss. Most authorities credit von Richthofen with the first triplane victory. At any rate, it is a matter of record that Werner Voss received his Fokker triplane (Fl-103/17) on the same day that Manfred von Richthofen received his (Fl-102/17), August 21, 1917, and that, on the following day, Voss scored a double victory.

Manfred von Richthofen, back at the front, was not the old Richthofen. His defeat and his stay in the hospital had taken away his aura of invincibility and he was not yet physically fit. He scored two victories, one of them very doubtful, and brought his tally to 59. He was aware of Voss again, who—once more—stood second to him on the roster of aces. He tried out his Fokker triplane on September 2, shooting down one of his favorite victims, an R.E. 8.

"It is a good ship," he said. "We will replace our Albatroses."

He scored one more victory in the triplane, then went on leave while the Fokker factory built triplanes for his *Jasta 11*. That month of September while he was away was a bad month for aces. The French lost Guynemer; Kurt Wolff, the Baron's old comrade who was now commanding *Jasta 11*, went down in flames and so did Höhndorf who had flown with Boelcke in the old Eindecker days.

Werner Voss looked at the Richthofen score of 60 and it did not seem out of reach. He had the open sky and good foes and nobody was holding him back. He no longer worried about his men. They had proved that they could take care of themselves.

On September 6 Voss scored his fortieth and forty-first victories. He scored three in one day on the tenth, another on the eleventh and still another on the twelfth; seven victories in seven days, six of them over Camels and S.E. 5s, the best fighters of the British Air Force.

The last victory was costly. A British Camel flight gave the Voss *Jasta* the worst licking that they had taken since coming to the front. Two of the triplanes were shot down and, in trying to save the second of them, Voss was boxed by two of the Camels. They poured 67 rounds into his ship before he succeeded in shooting one of them down and escaping from the trap. He landed with a bullet in his right bicep and a bad cut on his left eyebrow from his own shattered windscreen. The wounds were not serious but they sidelined him.

He had 47 victories and Manfred von Richthofen was resting with 61. Voss was only 14 victories behind and the doctors would not let him fly. He brooded as he paced the drome restlessly, sending other men out to fight and watching for them to come home. Honors and recognition meant more to him now than they had once. He had fought a long war.

On September 23, Werner Voss flew again.

Werner Voss as he appeared when he assumed command of *Jasta 10*. McCudden, the great British ace who served in every year of the war and met Germany's best, wrote of him: "His flying was wonderful . . . he was the bravest German airman . . . a privilege to see fight."
Society of WW I Aero Historians

The doctor permitted him to fly and test his arm, still in heavy bandages, but not to return to full duty as patrol leader.

Voss took off alone. The facts concerning this flight, what kind of day it was and what Voss saw, are well known. His enemies, a number of them, wrote the story and the record is complete.

It was the first time since he first adopted it, that Voss had flown without the checker identification on his wings, the insigne of the Death's-Head Hussars on his fuselage. His own ship had been badly damaged in his last fight and the new one had not been delivered. He flew a blue and silver triplane that belonged to one of his pilots.

Over the lines at 18,000 feet he saw a flight of Bristol Fighters approaching him. The Bristol was the toughest opponent on the front, a two-seater which performed like a fighter with two men fore and aft manning guns. He eyed the Bristols but did not approach them. There were six Bristols with 12 men and 18 guns. It was too much.

The day was amazingly clear at this height, with some cloud lower down. From his elevation he could see the French coastline, Dunkirk, Calais, Boulogne. There were two transports in the channel and two black destroyers. Beyond them he could see England, the white cliffs of Dover. As he banked, the spires of Amiens cathedral came into view. He could look into Holland and below him was Belgium.

Below him, too, were British planes. The British had copied the German pattern and were flying in circuses. Eight S.E.5s were patrolling under the Bristols. Under them were two flights of Camels. Tiny dots away down in the immensity were the observation planes, two flights of R.E.8s. The sky was full of English and not another German plane in sight.

Keeping an eye on the Bristols who were not in a position to attack him, Voss dropped down closer to the S.E.s, keeping the sun at his back. If they saw him, they would not consider him dangerous in himself but they might suspect that he was a decoy and be watching for other Germans. He edged closer and closer, then he swooped down.

It was the tactic that he had used so often; taking a large formation by surprise and picking out one plane for a quick kill. He poured a burst into the nearest S.E.5 and saw the Briton go down trailing smoke as he turned. He was too far east for the Bris-

An informal photograph of *Jagdstaffel 10*, Voss' famous triplane *Jasta*, as the pilots prepare for a patrol with the assistance of their mechanics.

tols, zooming away from the surprised companions of the ship he had downed.

The attack was perfectly executed, but luck was not with him. In all of that sky filled with British planes, there was still another flight, a flight of S.E.5s belonging to Squadron 56, the greatest British squadron of the war. They came out of the sun as he had and they blocked his escape route. To turn back meant meeting seven S.E.s, to dive meant that he would be surrounded by Camels. He did not know it but the flight that dived on him was composed of McCudden, Bowman, Mayberry, Hoidge and Rhys-Davids, five British aces. Jimmy McCudden later described the fight in his *Five Years in the Royal Flying Corps*.

"The Hun triplane was practically underneath our formation now," McCudden wrote, "so down we dived at colossal speed. I went to the right, Rhys-Davids to the left, and we got

National Archives

behind the triplane together. The German pilot turned in a most disconcertingly quick manner, not climbing nor making an Immelmann turn, but in a sort of flat, half spin. By now the German triplane was in the middle of our formation and its handling was wonderful to behold. The pilot seemed to be firing at all of us simultaneously and, although I got behind him a second time, I could hardly stay there for a second."

It was a tight trap but Voss shot his way out of it. He went through the great McCudden to get out, riddling his wings. He was in the clear for a matter of seconds but three S.E.s from the flight he had first attacked were between him and the only escape route. Their coming made the odds eight to one.

Lieutenant Rothesay Stuart Wortley, the pilot of one of the Bristols wrote of what happened then in *Letters from a Flying Officer*.

"For eight minutes on end he fought the eight," Wortley wrote, "while I sat 1,000 feet above, watching with profoundest admiration this display of skill and daring. The dexterity of his maneuvering was quite amazing. He was in and out and round about our scouts, zigzagging like forked lightning through the sky. None of our men could get at him. Then he broke off the fight and darted off to join a flight of Albatri [Albatroses] which had appeared upon the scene—and were hanging about some distance away as if hesitating to take part. Placing himself at the head of this formation he again wheeled to the attack. But the Albatri proved themselves unworthy of their would-be leader. They followed him to just within range of our machines and they turned and fled."

Werner Voss had shot his way out of a ring of eight S.E.s as he had out of the first five and he had his enemies scattered over several miles of sky. Concentrated as he was on his foes, he still spotted the Albatros flight when it appeared above him to the east of the Bristols and at about their level. He was able to shake off his enemies and zoom toward his friends, but he was battle-hot and in no mood for more escape. Rhys-Davids says that there were 11 Albatros scouts and as soon as Voss was certain that he had their attention, he turned back to attack the eight S.E.s, the four additional S.E.s climbing up to join them, and one of the Camel flights which was also climbing in the south. He was utterly reckless as far as the Bristols were concerned or he may have guessed that their orders were to stay on top unless their aid was urgently needed. Only one of the Albatros scouts followed him down.

Cowardly? Jimmy McCudden says not. "By this time," he wrote, a "red-nosed Albatros scout had arrived and was apparently doing its best to guard the triplane's tail. The formation of six Albatros scouts stayed above us and were prevented from diving on us by the arrival of a formation of Spads."

The Spads were the last fantastic touch. The whole Royal Flying Corps seemed to be concentrated now in that one section of the sky above Ypres. One of the S.E.s shot down the Albatros and the pilot's name is lost to history, a brave man who must have known that he didn't have a chance when he followed Voss.

"The triplane was still circling around in the midst of six S.E.s who were all firing at it as opportunity offered," McCudden wrote, "and at one time I noted the triplane in the apex of a cone of tracer bullets from at least five machines simultaneously, and each machine had two guns."

It could not continue indefinitely, of course. The Hussar had flown to his last battle and he must have known it but he never conceded.

"I got in several good bursts at the triplane without apparent effect," Rhys-Davids wrote in his combat report. "Twice I placed a new Lewis drum on my gun. Eventually I got east and slightly above the triplane, and made for it, and got in a whole Lewis drum and a corresponding number of Vickers into him. He made no attempt to turn until I was so close to him that I was certain that we would collide. He passed my right hand wing by inches and went down. . . ."

It was all over; the dreams, the ambitions, the rivalry, the restlessness, the impatience and the bravery. Werner Voss crashed into the earth on the English side of the lines where he had done most of his fighting. The English buried him and Jimmy McCudden wrote his epitaph.

"His flying was wonderful," he said, "his courage magnificent, and in my opinion he is the bravest German airman whom it has been my privilege to see fight." •

Georges Guynemer

The Fragile Knight

By William E. Barrett

O N THE morning of November 21, 1914 there was no joy in France. The German Army was hammering a weary French Army in a war that was a little over three months old. The fate of the channel ports was hanging in the balance, and with those ports the fate of France. In the town of Pau, Captain Bernard-Thierry was facing a few grim problems of his own. He was charged with recruiting for the French Air Service, a military branch lacking in tradition, in glory and, what was worse to a Frenchman, in logic.

Captain Bernard-Thierry needed no new problems, but he had one. An elegant and most vociferous young man had succeeded in talking his arrogant way past two stupid sentries and an inefficient secretary. He was standing before the Commander's desk.

"I make apologies," he said. "It was necessary that I see you. I must be accepted for the air service."

The Captain did not like his visitor's manner. He did not like the way in which the man had forced his way into his presence. He did not like his looks. Most emphatically he did not like his looks. Man? This creature looked more like a fainting girl; a thin, pale, girl with big brown eyes too large for a face that was almost pretty. "And why *must* you be accepted?" the Captain asked coldly.

The youth before him drew a deep breath. "I have been rejected by the army and the navy. France is fighting for her life and I am rejected. It is insupportable!"

Rejected by the army and the navy? But, of course. Why not? Captain Bernard-Thierry looked at his visitor with hard eyes. A child could push this tall, frail creature over. The sound of a shot would probably frighten him to death.

"Look you!" he said. "Am I then a hospital to take what is unfit to do a man's work? To fly takes courage."

"I have flown. I went up with an aviator when I was at school. I paid him.

"I do not ask to fly," the young man continued. "I am a student of engineering. I know combustion engines. I have taken them apart and put them together again. I will do anything if you will accept me, any kind of work that you have."

In his own mind, Captain Bernard-Thierry was reaching a decision. This was a lunatic service for which he recruited. The only men who could fly were mountebanks of one kind or another, daredevils of the acrobatic breed who before the war had performed in aeroplanes at country fairs; physical freaks, most of them, who would never look like soldiers in any kind of uniform. The mechanics were worse, much worse.

"What is your name?" he said.

The young man drew himself straight. "Georges Marie Ludovic Jules Guynemer."

"And your age?"

"Nineteen. I will be twenty on the twenty-fourth of December. Christmas Eve."

"I know when it occurs, the Eve of Christmas. And the name is too long. You are Georges Guynemer. I can enlist you as a private; an apprentice mechanic. Only that."

The pale face before him lighted up. "I thank you, my Captain. I have prayed for this."

It was November 21, 1914 and Georges

Richard Hardin

THE FRAGILE KNIGHT

Guynemer affixed his name to a paper which entitled him to one cent a day in a branch of the armed services that was without prestige. He was even lower than a private, since an apprentice mechanic was subject to the orders of privates.

Guynemer had been a puny baby and a weak boy. He was subject to colds and he had a delicate stomach that could digest only comparatively few foods, so he could not gain in weight or strength. Petted and babied by his mother and two older sisters when he was small, he had not been well enough to go to school, so a woman teacher had joined the household to teach him. His sisters were the only classmates he knew until he was 12. He had been surrounded by women, so he had learned the gestures and habits and intonations of women. Worse, he looked like his sisters. His father, a retired army officer, had done all that he could for him but Georges had lacked the strength to share his father's activities. He did, however, share his father's mind and will.

It had taken a strong will to survive the ordeal of going away to boarding school at 12 to live among the first boys he had ever known. He had been hazed and bullied and mistreated, but his strength was within him and he had permitted no one to break him. He did not permit the rough mechanics of the French Air Service to break him either.

They called him "Mademoiselle" from the start and they gave him the dirtiest jobs to do. They emptied buckets of dirty crankcase oil on him and they sent him on ridiculous errands and they kicked him even when he moved fast. He slept on a hangar floor and caught cold, ate coarse food and vomited, but he did not quit and he did not hold grudges. He knew more about engines than most of the mechanics and he knew what none of them knew—the laws of physics and mechanics.

U. S. Signal Corps

The Nieuport 27 (left) is one of the many planes flown by Guynemer. He won many combats in the Nieuport which was ideally adapted to his style of flying and fighting, but his name is usually associated with the Spad for which he had an even greater enthusiasm.

Georges Guynemer (right) was the idol of France. His 53 victories, although impressive, are not the measure of his greatness. He inspired the entire French Air Service by his daring exploits and was the hero of French schoolboys when the war was going badly for France. Guynemer never hesitated to attack balloons or troops on the ground or German railroad yards. "My aeroplane," he said, "is but a flying gun. It must go where it is most needed."

On January 26, 1915 Georges Guynemer was transferred to the flying school on the same drome at Pau where he had served as a mechanic apprentice. It was the fulfillment of a dream that he had never dared to express and neither recurring colds nor lack of physical stamina was permitted to interfere with it. He took to flight training with joy.

Guynemer soloed his first "Penguin" on February 1, 1915. The Penguin was a Blériot monoplane with clipped wings which would not rise from the ground. He moved to the second stage on February 7 and experienced the thrill of actually leaving the ground. On March 10 he flew above the field and hangars and confirmed for himself the fact that the air was his element. He left Blériots shortly after that and did his advance work on the Morane-Saulnier Parasol, the ship which was to be his first war plane.

Georges Guynemer flew a Parasol to Vauciennes on June 8, 1915, assigned as a corporal-pilot to Escadrille M.S. 3 under the command of Captain Brocard. This escadrille consisted of picked men, men whose names were destined to make the list of aces and heroes: Vedrines, Heurtaux, De La Tour, Dorme, Auger and Raymond. They were a hard-bitten crew and did not welcome a new member who was thin and "ladylike."

On his first flight over enemy lines Guynemer saw three German planes. The Germans were engaged in the same work as he was and that work did not include shooting at other planes. The Germans on the ground were a different matter. They did not like French observation which might direct artillery fire in their direction and they fired at French planes with every weapon they had. On his third patrol, June 16, 1915, Guynemer's ship was hit.

Guynemer felt the shock in the controls and his Morane went through one complete revolution before he leveled off, put his nose down and headed for home. There was a tap on his shoulder. His observer, Lieutenant de Lavolette, was frowning at him and pointing toward the right wing. The shell had made a small hole in the fabric but had obviously done no serious structural damage. Lieutenant de Lavolette had not finished his work. He did not want to go home. Guynemer shrugged. "The King is not my cousin," he said, "but it is your risk as well as mine."

He flew back over the guns. The "King is not my cousin" expression was a favorite of his, conveying his fatalistic belief that he would not receive any special favors from Fate or from people. On this occasion he flew coolly back and forth until his observer had completed his sketches, then flew him home. The incident made his reputation in Escadrille M.S. 3. He belonged. The following day he nailed that reputation down firmly. He came home with eight bullet holes in his ship and without any display of nerves.

Guynemer, however, did not like being fired upon by the Germans without firing back. He started experimenting with machine guns and machine gun mounts.

Earlier in the year, Roland Garros had created a brief sensation with his "secret weapon." The weapon was crude but effective. Garros attached steel deflection plates to the propeller of his plane so that he could fire a machine gun through the propeller arc. When Garros was forced to land behind German lines, his device provided the inspiration for Anthony Fokker's interrupter gear, and Oswald Boelcke had flown a plane equipped with it, a Fokker Eindecker, into action on June 30.

Guynemer and his squadron mates knew nothing of these developments, of course. They flew each day, making their observations under fire and seldom seeing an enemy plane. On July 19, 1915 Guynemer saw two. He was flying with an observer named Guerder who was as keen for combat as he was. They had a machine gun on a rigid rear cockpit mount. Guynemer chased the nearest German and maneuvered around him, trying to point his tail at him, but the German maneuvered too, and Guerder could not get a shot.

The second German plane, an Aviatik, circled around, interested in the combat, and Guynemer came up under him. The German observer leaned over the cockpit rim and fired at the French ship with a rifle. Guynemer banked steeply and nosed down. Guerder poured a burst from the machine gun into the mid-section of the German ship as the Morane's tail whipped around and the Aviatik plunged down in flames.

THE FRAGILE KNIGHT

M.S. 3 had a big celebration that night and command headquarters, recognizing that pilot and gunner had showed equal skill, awarded each of them the *Médaille Militaire* and credited each with an aerial victory.

It is an extraordinary thing that Guynemer stood up so staunchly to the daily demands of aerial warfare flying his tiny kite under constant fire without any improvement in his basic health and yet without any sign of strain. He still guarded himself from drafts more carefully than he guarded himself from bullets. he was careful of his diet, he rested whenever he could—and he was, perhaps, the thinnest, frailest looking soldier in the French service.

In September the first single-seater Nieuports reached the escadrille and its designation was changed to N-3. It adopted an insigne, too, and received the name that it was to carry into history. It became "The Stork Escadrille"—*Les Cigognes*. The French Air Force had finally recognized the need for fighters dedicated to the task of preventing the enemy from crossing the lines to bomb or observe. N-3 was the first such group and the Nieuport with which it was equipped had a Lewis gun mounted on the top center section so that it could be fired forward over the prop.

On December 5, 1915 Guynemer scored his first victory in a Nieuport, but he was flying alone and no ground observer witnessed the combat so he was not credited. Three days later he shot down an L.V.G. which flamed and there was no doubt tbout that one. He scored his third official on December 11 and his fourth on December 14 in one of the old Moranes on a reconnaissance mission with Bucquet as an observer. A Fokker caught him

Another photo of the famous Nieuport 27. It was also flown by aces René Fonck and Raoul Lufbery.

U. S. Army Air Corps

on the way home and riddled his ship, miraculously missing both pilot and observer. It was Guynemer's first encounter with the Fokker Eindecker and its synchronized machine gun, and he was lucky to escape alive. His Morane collapsed on landing.

On Christmas Eve 1915, his twenty-first birthday, Georges Guynemer was decorated with The Cross of the *Légion d'Honneur*. The French Air Force had destroyed a total of 15 German planes in the last three months of 1915 and Guynemer had accounted for three of those 15 within a single week.

On February 21, Germany let loose the most terrific bombardment in the history of the world. For nine solid hours the guns hammered the lines before Verdun. The trenches were obliterated, railroads wiped out, towns reduced to powder. Behind a continuing barrage on February 22, 300,000 German troops advanced to the attack. The Germans fired an estimated 1,000,000 high explosive shells a day for four days, and on the fourth day, the German troops entered Fort Douaumont, the key fortress of Verdun. The French, however, were tough and when they launched a massive counteroffensive on February 27 under General Pétain, the Germans knew, and the world knew, that the fight for Verdun would be a long, hard siege.

Far to the south, the Stork Escadrille found itself on a relatively quiet front, and although they were scoring many victories now with the Nieuport, they were more interested in the fate of Verdun than in their own daily round. They cheered when their orders came transferring them to the Verdun front in March. Guynemer was jubilant. He had eight victories and only one French pilot, Navarre, had more.

"We shall see who commands the air," he said. "It will now be different."

He flew over the Verdun front for the first time on March 15, 1916 and he did not have to hunt far. German planes were everywhere. He had seen Fokker Eindeckers but he had never seen the Fokker D-1 or the Halberstadt, biplane single-seaters which, like the Fokker Eindecker, fired forward. The first biplane he saw was too fast for him and he was in the pilot's sights before he could maneuver. Lead slammed into his cockpit and the windscreen exploded in his face. There was blood in his eyes and his left side seemed paralyzed. His Nieuport spun down out of

Guynemer abandoned the Nieuport for the Spad (right) after his first patrol in a Spad 7. He continually harassed the Spad engineers with his ideas for improving the ship, the most notorious being a mounting which fitted a small 37 mm cannon between the blocks of a geared Hispano-Suiza engine so that the shell could be fired through the propeller shaft. Spad engineers built the so-called "Cannon Spad" for Guynemer under protest. It was never notably successful, though Fonck and others tried it.

THE FRAGILE KNIGHT

the sky and he pulled out of the spin, by blind instinct, a few hundred feet above the ground. He landed at Brocourt and they lifted him, unconscious, from the cockpit.

There were two bullets in Guynemer's left arm and a fragment of the aluminum windscreen was imbedded in his jaw, a fragment which the surgeons never succeeded in removing. He had a cut in his eyelid, three gashes in his face and a wound in his scalp.

When Guynemer became fully aware of his surroundings, he was in a Paris hospital.

This, he thought, was an end to glory. He was needed at Verdun and he had failed. His depression was very deep for days. Then his will asserted itself and he struggled against hospital restraint. He returned to his squadron on April 26 against the protests of the doctors, more of a ghost than ever, thinner than ever, and with a bandage still on his left arm.

The proud Storks, he learned, had been all but annihilated on their first two days in the air above Verdun. Captain Brocard still commanded but he looked older and sadder.

"Assign me a ship," Guynemer said. "I must fly again."

"Impossible. You are not fit."

"I will be fit for nothing else until I do."

The Captain was wise in the ways of war

French Official

GEORGES GUYNEMER

pilots. He knew the compulsion that drove a brave man back to battle after a defeat, but he believed, too, that a pilot who has been shot down in combat is like a prize fighter who has been knocked out in the ring. He has lost his feeling of invincibility and with that he has lost his best protection against death.

Still, when a man knows that and insists upon going back, what is one to do? Captain Brocard spread his hands wide.

"As you will, my comrade," he said. "You have been missed."

Georges Guynemer took off alone six weeks after he was shot down. He flew his Nieuport toward the lines and the first German he met was to be his personal test of fitness. It was a Rumpler, a two-seater. The pilot was equipped with a front-firing gun and the observer manned another in the rear cockpit. Guynemer was above them and he dived.

Spads were not completely invincible. The one below lost the aerial argument with the enemy.

THE FRAGILE KNIGHT

The resultant combat was witnessed by hundreds of French soldiers on the ground and it was the strangest aerial combat of the war.

Guynemer came down to the Rumpler head-on. The observer was tense behind his gun, expecting the normal attack technique. For a split second Guynemer held the pilot in his sights but did not fire. The German pilot, taken by surprise, was slow in manning his gun and when he fired, Guynemer was no longer a target; he was diving beneath the two-seater. He came out of his dive to zoom toward the Rumpler's blind spot as the nose of the German came down. He had a no deflection shot and he held his fire. The German pilot was seeking another shot at him and Guynemer evaded him to concentrate his attack upon the rear gunner who fired burst after burst at him without hitting him.

For long minutes the strange combat continued while the awed spectators on the ground watched and wondered. Guynemer in his Nieuport was a flashing, elusive insect buzzing around his larger foe, feinting an attack upon the front gun, then half rolling to worry the gunner, coming back under the blind spot and hanging there on his prop while the German tried to shake him off.

At length the German pilot was convinced, as were those on the ground, that this mad Frenchman's guns were jammed. He put his nose down, risking straight line flight to streak for home. Guynemer let him go.

Two of the Storks had taken off from the drome to rescue their comrade with jammed guns, responding to messages from front line observers, but Guynemer did not know that. He landed on his home base and made his way on shaky legs to a cot. He was lying there, sick, spent and exhausted, when Captain Brocard came to him.

"I killed those Huns a dozen times," Guynemer said, "and they must have fired five hundred rounds without hitting me once. I am content."

Only once did he speak of that strange combat on April 26, 1916. "That was the decisive moment of my life," he said. "I had to conquer myself. The Boche was nothing."

The war moved along while Guynemer went on leave to Compiègne. The Germans still pounded doggedly at Verdun but the first force and fury of their drive was spent. The French hung on stubbornly and the war of attrition drained both sides while the British moved a new army of 2,000,000 men to France for their big offensive on the Somme.

Georges Guynemer returned to the Storks on May 18, 1916 in the finest physical condition of his life. He was still thin as he would always be, but he was stronger, less susceptible to colds, eager to be back in action with his new rank of *Sous-Lieutenant*.

The Storks had suffered heavily and many of the old comrades were gone, but good men had taken their places. There was a new Nieuport of better performance and the top center-section mounting of the Lewis gun had been improved.

Strangely, the Allies had not yet succeeded in perfecting any kind of a workable interrupter gear to permit firing a machine gun through the prop, although the Germans had had the device for over a year. The English were flying pusher type planes with the engine behind the pilot in order to obtain front fire, and the French still fired over the propeller.

Guynemer had satisfied himself on the question of his own fitness to fight, but the commander of his escadrille compelled him to take his time, to break in gently. Not until June 18 did he have a combat over the lines and on that day he blasted one of the new Fokker scouts out of the air in less than one minute.

It was Guynemer's only victory on the Verdun front. The British launched their big offensive on the Somme on July 1, 1916 and the Storks went into action with the British squadrons.

The bad luck which had greeted his first appearance on the Verdun front was waiting for Guynemer on the Somme. On July 6 a Fokker shot him down and he made his own drome with two cut cables, eight bullet holes in his Nieuport and one bullet hole in his flight jacket. Instead of accepting this as a challenge to his feeling of invincibility, he proclaimed it a proof that no German could kill him. He flew every day of that blazing month and although he was credited with only two official victories (his tenth and eleventh), he was certain that he had obtained many more. On July 27 he fought an epochal battle with three two-seaters and the seven Albatroses which dived to their rescue, escaping from the trap with incredible skill.

In this combat, Guynemer received 86 bullets in his Nieuport. He landed with a punctured gasoline tank, a bullet in the oil reservoir, two bullets wedged in the gun mount, one in his cartridge case, one in the back of his seat, one in the rudder, a dozen in the wings and one—obviously spent after passing through some part of his plane—in his glove where it had bruised his finger without breaking the skin. Ten enemies had been shooting at him, had hit him 86 times, and had failed to bring him down.

When the new Spad appeared in September, Guynemer received one of the first two as his personal ship. The Spad looked more German than French and it broke with French tradition which had favored the light maneuverable ship with a light engine. The Spad was heavy, solidly constructed, and powered with the 150-horsepower Hispano-Suiza engine. It had a span of 25 feet, eight inches, was 20 feet in over-all length and weighed 1,100 pounds empty. Of prime importance, it was the first French ship with a synchronized gun.

Flying the Spad, Guynemer doubled his score in the course of a few months. He ended 1916 with 25 victories, the unchallenged leader of all French aces.

The Storks transferred to Lorraine in February 1917 after six months fighting on the Somme, and Guynemer scored the first victory on the new front by shooting down a three-place German Gotha. He had scored five victories in January, so this was his thirty-first.

March 16, 1917 was one of the big days of Guynemer's life. He was promoted to Captain and received from President Poincairé of France the Russian decoration, the Cross of Saint George, which the Czar awarded him for his tremendous contribution to the Allied cause. Before the ceremonies Guynemer flew out on solo patrol and shot down a Roland pursuit ship and two two-seaters, the first triple victory scored by a French pilot.

Germany moved back into command of the air during that month of March 1917. The Albatros D-3 made its appearance with two machine guns synchronized to fire through the prop. It was the most destructive plane of the war to date. The British bore the brunt of the attack by the Albatros circuses which in April—Bloody April—shot down five British planes for every German lost. The French, however, also lost heavily, particularly observation planes since theirs were markedly inferior to the Germans'.

It was a difficult time for the French government and the French Air Service, but Guynemer's personal star was still rising. He had 37 victories on May 1 and only one rival, Captain Albert Ball of the Royal Flying Corps, a reckless, headlong pilot of his own type with whom he was often compared. Ball's score was higher than Guynemer's and he too seemed invincible. On May 7, a foggy, windy day, Guynemer scored his thirty-eighth victory and Ball disappeared. The great English pilot was last seen chasing a German plane in a dark, cloudy sky. Neither his body nor his plane was ever found.

"He was not defeated," Guynemer said, "nor shot down by a German; he was merely lost in the air as a ship is lost at sea. It is the perfect ending."

Before the month was over he had equaled Ball's score. He had four victories in one day on May 25 and another the next day, his forty-third. His score continued to mount during June, and on July 28, 1917 on the Ypres front, he reached the magic number of 50.

There was no greater personality in France then, not even among the great generals. Girls, hundreds of them, wrote Guynemer love letters, schoolboys collected pictures of him and yearned to be like him. He had every decoration that France could bestow, including the Commander of the *Légion d' Honneur*, and he had decorations from the other Allied powers. He owned a sporty white roadster in which he drove frequently to Paris for consultation with the Spad engineers. He should have been spoiled and conceited and impossible, but he wasn't. At the height of his glory he was probably more humble than at any time in his life.

THE FRAGILE KNIGHT

Always devoutly religious, he spent much time on every Paris visit in the Church of Saint Pierre de Chaillot which he had adopted as his parish church. He attended Masses when he could and he was a familiar figure to the regular parishioners, kneeling alone before the altar, unaware of anyone else.

The Stork Escadrille was fighting on the Ypres front in Flanders where the Germans were driving to capture the channel ports of Calais and Dunkirk. The fighting was heavy on land and in the air. Guynemer scored his fifty-first, fifty-second and fifty-third victories in August and was beginning to show the strain. He caught a cold which he could not shake off and Captain Heurtaux, who had commanded the Storks since Brocard moved up to the rank of major and the post of attaché to the minister of aeronautics, tried in vain to remove him from duty until he was rested.

On September 3 Heurtaux was wounded and Guynemer succeeded him in command.

The French Air Force was being completely reorganized and there were rumors that the day of the individualist was over, that the French were going to match the Germans with huge formations of fighters. This worried Guynemer who saw no role for himself as a member of a "circus." He flew and fought alone and it was the only way that he could fly and fight.

This picture, in which Guynemer is wearing his medals, was taken at the Spad factory during one of his many visits. The Spad engineers were, no doubt, relieved when Guynemer left.

Legend states that the great German ace Oswald Boelcke (above) engaged in combat with Guynemer. They did fly and fight on the same fronts at about the same time, but if there was a duel between the two there is no record of it and it is doubtful that they ever met in the air. Boelcke and Guynemer were, however, aware of each other and were, in a sense, rivals.

There were other rumors; that he was to be removed from the front to a strategy board, that he was to be adviser to the Americans in training their fighter pilots, that he was to be sent on a tour of the United States to stimulate interest in aviation. At any rate, when he was informed that his old commander, Major Brocard, and Major du Peuty, Chief of Aviation, were to visit the Stork Escadrille on the morning of September 11, he was nervous, upset and in a very strange mood for him: morose, brooding, ill-tempered.

The drome was heavy with fog on the morning of the proposed visit. Guynemer was out at dawn, impatient with the weather, irritated because his Cannon Spad was again in need of repairs. When the fog lifted a little, shortly before 8:00 a.m., he called *Sous-Lieutenant* Bozon-Verduraz.

"We will fly a patrol," he said.

Bozon-Verduraz was aghast. "But, my Captain," he said. "the dignitaries will arrive at nine."

"We will have time for a patrol."

Guynemer was curt. He led the other plane into the clearing sky, flying his old Spad which he called *"Le Vieux Charles."* He flew out over the sea and then southeast to Langemarck. He crossed the German lines before he saw the two-seater below him. He signaled Bozon-Verduraz and dived down, coming recklessly into the German pilot, head-on, which was not the way to fight two-seaters of late 1917. The German fired one burst and spun to his right. Guynemer overshot him, banked fast and came back, following him down.

That was all that Bozon-Verduraz saw. There was a German fighter flight in the air above him and Bozon-Verduraz streaked north, drawing them away from Guynemer. The Germans followed him but, probably wary that he was a decoy drawing them into a trap, did not come down on him. When he had lost them, Bozon-Verduraz returned to the point where he had left Guynemer but there was no sign of his commander or of the plane he had pursued, either in the air or on the ground. The young pilot continued his patrol of the area until he was low on petrol, then he flew home.

Guynemer had not returned.

He never did return. The Storks kept a long vigil of waiting and phones were hot along the front seeking news of him, but there was no news. The Germans released no victorious dispatches as they certainly would have had they brought the great Guynemer down. What had happened to him?

After the French, reluctantly, released the news that Guynemer was missing, a German pilot named Wissemann claimed that he had shot Guynemer down. He stated, however, that the date was the tenth, so his claim meant nothing.

The mystery of Guynemer's fate remained and his own remark on the death of Ball was recalled. He too had disappeared, not under German guns, but merely "lost in the air as a ship is lost at sea."

It would be dramatic and romantic to end his story thus, but the Germans ultimately supplied a less romantic answer. Guynemer, they said, had been brought down south of Poelcapelle cemetery and a surgeon from an infantry battalion had examined his body. He had been shot through the forehead, and the forefinger of his left hand had been shot off. He had a broken arm and a broken leg. The area was under heavy artillery fire, the report added. The surgeon who examined the body and the men who accompanied him were compelled to leave the body of Guynemer beside his plane. They, too, were dead now and the whole area had been flattened by the artillery fire. Presumably Guynemer and his *Le Vieux Charles* had been pounded into the clay by the same barrage. Only the record remained, the hastily written memo of a methodical German surgeon who was under fire when he wrote it; a man with only a few more minutes of his own life left to live.

The record ends there and the French have never accepted the German postscript as true. Georges Guynemer scored 53 victories, officially, in the air. Before the war was over there were aces who topped that score, but under different conditions. No one in France reached Guynemer's pinnacle of fame, of public acclaim that was close to adoration. He stood there, and stands there still, alone. Till this day the children of France enjoy the legend that Guynemer never died—he just flew so high he could never come down. •

Raoul Lufbery
Ace of the Lafayette

By William W. Walker

THE crumbling records of the devil-may-care Lafayette Escadrille list his name at the top with 18 officially confirmed victories. What kind of man was this legendary figure who is virtually forgotten today?

The story of Raoul Lufbery, born in France in 1885 of an American father and French mother, is a twentieth century odyssey. It was a restless pilgrimage to the far corners of the earth in search of adventure, a quest for whatever destiny might bring. Insatiable wanderlust took him from his boyhood home in Connecticut to Europe, to the Far East and finally back to his native France where a flaming "finis" was emblazoned on a gallant career.

Deprived of his parents when his mother died and his father returned to America, Lufbery was reared by his grandparents in France. Formal schooling was not to his taste and the restlessness in him prevailed. He went to live in America, but the leisurely pace of life in rural Wallingford bored him. At the age of 17 he ran away from home. The whole world was his oyster and he resolved to see what it offered in the way of high adventure.

He roamed through France for several years, waiting on table in a Greek restaurant, working as a dock stevedore, finally learning the hazardous trade of dirt track auto racer. Algiers beckoned next, followed

RAOUL LUFBERY

by stops in Tunis, Egypt, Bulgaria, South America and a stint in the German merchant marine. He made a trip home where he expected to find his father, but fate played a cruel trick on him. The elder Lufbery, unaware that his son was returning home, had sailed for France a few hours prior to Raoul's arrival. Their paths never crossed again.

Sorely disappointed and heartsick, Raoul's restless footsteps led him to New Orleans where he enlisted in the U. S. Army. He served his two year hitch, from 1907 to 1909, in the Philippine Islands where he earned the reputation as the best rifle marksman in his regiment—a skill that was to pay off handsomely a decade later in France. His enlistment up, Lufbery explored the remote nooks and corners of the world that he hadn't yet visited. China and Japan were next on the schedule, followed by a trip to India.

Many years later his escadrille crony, Bert Hall, described Raoul as "that traveling man. Why, you could name damn near any city or place from Marseille to Singapore and back to Bombay—Lufbery had been there. He'd sampled his share of the national grog, knew the mayor (and the mayor's daughter) intimately. He could tell you what the meteorological, wind and flying conditions were and when the trains left. He knew from personal experience how crowded and filthy the jails were, how the police treated street brawlers and if the jail food was fit to eat. He knew the world, men and life, not from reading it out of a book, but from having sampled it first hand."

R. R. Martin

Marc Pourpe, his flying mentor and patron, described Luf as ". . . a walking encyclopedia, always searching for practical information." He had a catalogue type mind that could recall the day, hour and very minute of anything important that happened in his life.

A stopover in Saigon, Cochin China in 1911 proved to be the turning point in his life. A new friend beckoned him to his ultimate career—flying. An excited crowd of natives milling around an ungainly contraption attracted Lufbery just like a magnet attracts iron. With the savoir-faire of a seasoned man of the world, he pushed closer to the center of excitement. It was an airplane, the first he'd ever seen, an old Blériot. Brushing the jabbering coolies aside, he confronted a harassed European attired in cavalry breeches, leather jacket, flying helmet and dusty boots.

"Monsieur! Raoul Lufbery *à vôtre service.*"

"Monsieur Lufbery? *Mon Dieu!* Can you make these idiots understand? I am Marc Pourpe and I am a stunt flyer. But my career will soon be over if I do not find shelter for my airplane before this cursed storm strikes. My mechanic has been taken ill, and I cannot make these heathens understand! They comprehend nothing! I must build a hangar! What am I to do?"

"Monsieur Pourpe, I can handle these fellows. Permit me to help."

Eagerly Pourpe accepted Lufbery's offer. Through the liberal use of harsh language (he

U. S. Air Service

Raoul Lufbery in his French uniform. A restless soldier of fortune before the war, he teamed up with stunt flyer Marc Pourpe. He became a mechanic in the French Air Service, piloted a Voisin bomber, then joined the Lafayette. He scored 17 victories before finally being shot down in flames.

Lufbery's first aviation experience was with stunt flyer Marc Pourpe who barnstormed in a prewar Blériot like that shown at left. Pourpe and Lufbery roamed the world putting on exhibition flights. Lufbery considered Pourpe his mentor and patron and vowed to avenge him when he was killed.

could swear in a dozen tongues), Lufbery quickly had the coolies organized and the hangar was built. Pourpe, impressed with this display of ability and highly grateful, offered Lufbery the job of traveling with him as his mechanic. Thus began his close association with the premier French stunt flyer and barnstormer.

Quick to learn, Lufbery soon proved to be an invaluable assistant to Pourpe on his crowd gathering aerial circus tour of the Far East. His amazing grasp of mechanics, his adaptable good humor and razor-sharp memory soon endeared him to Pourpe. The partnership was a living reincarnation of Damon and Pythias. Pourpe, in a literal sense, became the father who had been denied Lufbery all his life. For three years this perfectly matched team thrilled crowds in India and the Orient with their startling aerial exhibitions.

Many adventures marked their tour of the Orient, and one night in a small Chinese village, they nearly came to an untimely end. As Pourpe finished his exhibition and rolled his ship to a halt, the curious Chinese thronged around the Blériot. They gestured excitedly as they crowded around the ship, examining and investigating this strange contraption. After due consideration, they decided their reputations as master kite builders were in danger from these white foreign devils. With prolonged labor and application, they brought forth an exact replica built of bamboo sticks and gaudy paper. Excitedly they watched as it soared through the air just like a bird. But something was wrong. It did not "sing" as it went through the air. Perfectionists that they were, they jammed a large box full of angry, droning hornets into the flimsy device. It did make a buzzing sound as they sent it through the air, but it still did not sing and whine like the cursed foreigners' machine.

Prolonged harangues by the village hotheads convinced the Chinese that the two white men should die for the mysterious sorcery that produced a kite they could not duplicate. Warned by a friendly servant, Pourpe and Luf were lucky to make a twilight escape with an angry mob howling for their heads as the Blériot caromed down a pasture and finally became air-borne.

Next on the schedule of the intrepid team was Pourpe's epic flight from Cairo to

A French Voisin bomber like that shown below was the ship in which Raoul Lufbery first flew to war. He was assigned to Escadrille de Bombardment VB. 106 in 1915, flew Voisins for six months.

National Archives

Khartoum, Egypt, and return. Lufbery doggedly followed or preceded him on every stage of the journey, traveling by Nile steamers and cargo rafts, on camels and donkeys, by train and many times on foot, with his tools and a knapsack of food on his back.

The summer of 1914 found them in France inspecting a new plane. When the war broke out, Pourpe lost no time in volunteering his services. For the first time in three years the inseparable flying team faced the grim prospect of being parted. Pourpe was detailed for training at an observation school.

Lufbery tried vainly to enlist, but found that the only way, since he was only half French by ancestry, was by going through the ritual of joining the French Foreign Legion. Hardly had he made the shift to Escadrille N. 23 as a mechanic to his patron when Pourpe was killed in action on December 2, 1914. A grieving Lufbery swore a mighty oath to avenge Pourpe. The only way to get back at the hated Germans was to become a fighter pilot. And he resolved to do so, but for many months this ambition was frustrated.

With only a few weeks of training, he supplemented his knowledge earned in his association with Pourpe and received a flying certificate. He was posted to Escadrille de Bombardment VB. 106. Flying a lumbering Voisin bomber offered few chances for revenge on the hated Boche, but he flew his slow, clumsy ship deep over German lines on hazardous bombing and observation flights every day that the weather would allow. He never complained or seemed uneasy, even when his plane was shredded by ground fire.

Always his request was the same. "Please give me a transfer to *chasse* training." After constant harassment, his superior officer granted his request.

It was a curious paradox, in view of his later mastery of aerial acrobatics, that at first he was a complete failure as a student on the tricky little fighters. He flew with a heavy hand and would crack up his planes with almost precise regularity. Although he possessed a lightning quick mind and hair trigger reflexes, the French instructors almost despaired of making him a *pilote de chasse*. "That Lufbery," they shrugged, "lead handed, good only for a bomber pilot. For *chasse*, no, no." But with a single goal in mind, the deter-

Another view of the 1915 Voisin. They were slow, clumsy lumbering ships powered by a pusher engine. As a Voisin pilot, Lufbery found little of the revenge he was seeking against the Germans.

National Archives

RAOUL LUFBERY

mined Lufbery stubbornly refused to quit. With an iron will and constant application he overcame his shortcomings and became a complete master of combat flying.

His associates in the Lafayette Escadrille credited this burning desire to avenge Pourpe as the spark that carried him over all obstacles. It seemed that with Pourpe's death every other emotion temporarily died in Luf.

Those who flew with him appreciated his dexterity and believed that few flyers could equal him, that none could surpass him. His incomparable mastery of acrobatics did not come easy. He was not a natural born flyer like some, but literally pulled himself up by his own bootstraps. The plane eventually became an integral part of him, something that could be said of very few airmen.

Lufbery's official score of 17 planes was but a fractional part of his one man tornado of destruction. Many fights and victories took place so far back of German lines that confirmation was impossible. Week after week his plane would show the terrible scars of a savage duel. His official reports were terse, and that ended that day's crusade of revenge.

He cared but little for the credit. It was the inner satisfaction he felt after chalking up another tally in honor of Pourpe that was important to him. When he cashed his chips in a final blaze of glory, he was the oldest American pilot on the front and one of the war's greatest aces, in a class with Fonck, Bishop, Guynemer, Richthofen, Barker, Udet, Mannock and the others who emblazoned their names across the western front.

April 20, 1916 was a memorable day in the aerial history of World War I. That afternoon the *L'Escadrille Américaine,* soon to become world famous as the Lafayette Escadrille and as glamorous as Teddy Roosevelt's Rough Riders were in '98, was formed at a flying field at Luxeuil-les-Bains in the Vosges mountains. It was the culmination of over a year of dreams, toil, delays and outright opposition. Seven pilots received their orders, and from this nucleus was formed the original squadron. They were Bert Hall, Bill Thaw, Norman Prince, Kiffin Rockwell, Elliot Cowdin, Victor Chapman and Jimmy McConnell. The anxious young volunteers

Raoul Lufbery in the cockpit is about to take off from the Lafayette drome at Cachy in his Nieuport 27. Capt. R. Soubiran is looking at the camera, and Lt. Didier Masson is playing with Whiskey, the lion cub mascot of the escadrille. Prominent is the whooping Indian insigne of the unit.

U. S. Air Force

were sent to the quiet Vosges sector to acquire the teamwork necessary to a smoothly operating combat unit.

Early in 1915, two Americans, Norman Prince, who had a smattering of aviation training while in college, and William Thaw, daring hydroplane pilot, both of whom had entered the French Air Service through the Foreign Legion, determined to found an all American flying corps. A year later this organization became the Lafayette Escadrille. The mounting fame of Lufbery prompted an invitation for him to join the American unit, and he became a Lafayette pilot shortly after the group reached Verdun, on May 24, 1916.

Each volunteer was assigned his own sleek, speedy Nieuport scout powered by a 90 horsepower Le Rhône rotary motor. Armament consisted of a single Lewis gun mounted on the top wing, since prop-synchronized guns were not in use on Allied planes then. The Nieuports were maneuverable little crafts with an approximate speed of 115 mph. Two mechanics were assigned to each plane, and they took a fierce, Gallic pride in the exploits of the pilot they served.

Volunteers in the French Army started as second-class soldiers and automatically advanced to corporals when brevetted as military aviators. The frugal French operated on the theory that commissions had to be earned by deeds of valor or sheer length of service. Lufbery was the only volunteer other than Bill Thaw to earn a commission in the escadrille.

In May the escadrille was installed on their brand-new field on a large hill overlooking the beautiful Meuse Valley. A magnificent villa between town and their field was assigned to them as living quarters, and for a while life was not too arduous. Then, as they took their regular rotation of flying chores, they began to get a real taste of war and the perils of "Archy."

The first battle of Verdun was mounting to a crescendo of mass slaughter, and French aerial forces were bracing for a climactic struggle. Lufbery reported for duty and, for two years until his death in May 1918, rode the skyways over France and Germany like an avenging demon. The ham-handed bomber pilot had developed into one of the greatest aces of the war, a pilot whose attack was rapier swift, whose marksmanship was uncanny.

Lufbery and his gaudily painted Nieuport were in the air every day. "She's as trim and as saucy as a Paris mannikin parading down the Champs Élysées at Easter," was the way he described his ship. He probed deeper and deeper over enemy lines, looking for a taste of German blood. He scored his first official victory on July 30 in a singlehanded battle over Etain on the Verdun front. It was confirmed by French observers. Flushed with his initial killing, he went out scouting again late the same day, and over almost the identical sector scored another victory, the first double ever recorded in the French Air Service.

A double victory called for liquid celebration, and that night Luf was drinking Manhattans as fast as squadron mate Bert Hall could mix them. After three pitchers had found their mark, Luf was in a fighting mood and ready to take on a comrade in arms. "Come on, Bertie, let's rout out old Gitchy-Goomie. Let's kick the hell outta that miserable, boot licking disgrace to the uniform," he shouted, collapsing a rickety table with an emphatic whack.

"Now, Raoul, calm down," soothed Hall. "Sure, he's rubbed you the wrong way. I hate his guts, but you just don't haul off and hit a superior officer because you've had a few belts. Save your bile for the Krauts." Luf did just that.

On August 8, 1916 he scored his third victory and earned a citation for bravery. He acknowledged the bar of bright ribbon and brass in characteristic fashion by shooting down his fourth German, this one in flames, the following week. This splendid show of prowess won him promotion to the rank of adjutant.

Such intrepid flying also gained him a respite from the grim business of killing. Luf took a furlough, leaving his mates to carry on the war while he went to Chartres to wine, dine and forget war in the soft arms of a lady friend. Several mornings later a distress call came into squadron headquarters. The telegram was phrased in Lufbery's understated, to-the-point manner: "Please send a delegation to get me out of the local jailhouse. I am in Chartres and the stubborn gendarmes will not listen to reason."

That afternoon Captain Thenault buzzed Chartres. "What have you stupid pigs done with the leading member of the Lafayette Escadrille? A man with four victories! The immediate release of Adjutant Lufbery is most essential to the successful conduct of the war. Have him back by morning or heads will roll."

The next morning a bruised, disheveled but exuberant *pilote de chasse* returned. Aided and abetted by a jug of brandy and cheered on by the four doxies he had accumulated in his bar-hopping tour of Chartres, he got into a slight fracas with the M.P.s at the railway station. He downed four of them before he was overpowered by sheer weight of numbers. At the jail he went into action again and decked several more of his erstwhile allies. He was always looking for a good brawl, whether it was in the air, in a bar or in some dark alley, and after fifteen years of bumming around the world, he was handy with his fists. His story was as terse as his telegram. "I punched and they fell. Then the bastards locked me up. But I didn't start the fight. They did. I only finished it."

Lufbery was squat, chunky and steel muscled, just five feet six inches tall. His broad forehead was set off by deep, brooding eyes and a saucy mustache. Often his speech carried overtones of a strange accent that was a distillation of all the foreign tongues he'd been exposed to. Boisterous at times, Lufbery could keep his real inner self shut up like a clam in a shell, and to the men who slept, drank, brawled and fought beside him for two years, Lufbery was one of the great enigmas of the war.

He flew alone most of the time, patiently searching for the right opportunity to clobber a Hun. His mechanic's training asserted itself in the precise personal attention he accorded his engine. He labored for hours over his gun to obviate the chance of jam and had his ammo triple calibrated so an oversize shell

Lafayette Escadrille

wouldn't jam the breech. He had an uncanny faculty for watching everything that transpired in the swirling, bullet-laced maelstrom of a dogfight, often sacrificing a sure kill to extricate some green youngster from a tight spot. Twisting and turning, executing what came to be known as the squirrel cage maneuver, firing short staccato bursts at first one German, then another, he could play havoc with an entire enemy formation.

He showed very little elation in victory after his initial taste, and, conversely, no disappointment in defeat. Death held no terrors for him, and often he came back from combat patrol with his ship riddled like a sieve. He would shrug it off and complain: "Those damn Krauts must use armor plate or sky hooks to stay up. I gave 'em every piece of lead in my drums."

His remorseless hunt for Huns led him to battle with the first of the great German aces, Oswald Boelcke. Zooming and spiraling, pouring deadly streams of hot lead into each other, the two masters groped for advantage in great bursts of speed. Black bullet holes began to rip Luf's wings, guy wires twanged and struts melted into thin air. Two bullets pierced his flying suit, and one tore a gaping hole in his fur lined boot. The two gladiators fought to the point of sheer exhaustion, then with ammunition drums empty, they broke off the fight with salutes of mutual respect. Luf's tiny Nieuport was quivering with the strain and threatening to collapse under him at any moment, and he nursed it back to the field. As he carefully set it down the strain became too much and the shattered aircraft fell to pieces.

Decorations and citations fought for space on his lapel. There was the Military Cross from England. Alongside was the most prized and also the most difficult to earn—the *Médaille Militaire* from France. The citation for the *Croix de Guerre* read:

Lufbery, Raoul Sergeant Pilot of Escadrille N-124, Model of skill, of sang-froid, of courage. Has distinguished himself by long-range bombardments and daily combats in which he has engaged enemy planes. The 30th of July, he did not hesitate to attack at close range a group of four enemy planes. Brought down one of them in close proximity to our lines. Succeeded in bringing down a second the same day. This citation carries with it the Croix de Guerre with palm.

(Signed) *Joffre*

Simplicity was one of his finest qualities. He knew that he was a national hero and that the newspapers in France and America were full of his exploits. Yet he was never one to boast or take credit for himself.

A change of scenery to the Somme sector furnished the lads of the escadrille with more than their quota of daily combats. On December 27 Luf got two planes with only one being officially credited. His tenth victory was typical of the precise way in which he planned every flight.

Cruising alone at 18,000 feet, he encountered a couple of two-seater recon planes and five fighters. Carefully putting himself between the sun and his prey, he waited for a straggler to leave the compact formation.

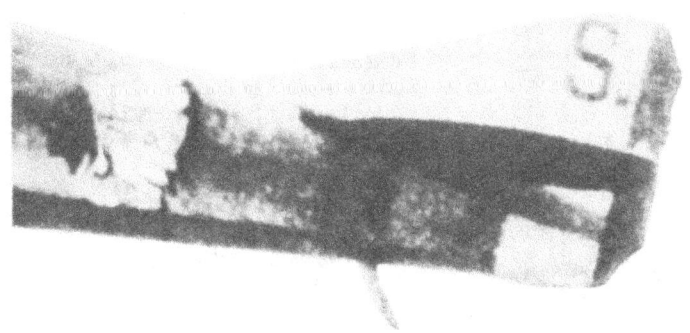

Whooping Indian patrol: A rare photograph of a Lafayette Escadrille Spad in actual flight taken during 1917. The Indian head insigne of the Lafayette was painted in various color combinations, usually with a reddish face and black feather tips.

Soon his chance came, and as he closed to less than 100 yards away, his finger tightened on the firing button. His gun jammed after a scant 30 rounds, but his precision aim had saved the day. Suddenly the German plane staggered, lurched back and forth crazily, and started its final, agonizing plunge to earth, both wings peeling off like strips of paper.

Lufbery had his own particular way of getting a two-seater. There was a blind spot on both sides of the front gun that offered the safest target, but as an alternative he would pull up underneath in one operation and stitch both cockpits with lead before the rear gunner could go into action over the sides. Lufbery would expound, "That rear Hun is a mighty G . . . damn mean bastard, and he's not to be trusted. The stings he puts in those twin Spandaus are just a prelude to the band playing the funeral march."

One balmy afternoon, an English officer from a neighboring squadron approached Bert Hall, Lufbery, Norman Prince, Kiffin Rockwell, Bill Thaw and other escadrille members with a friendly suggestion:*

"What say, you bloody Yanks, let's call off the war and drink up."

The Americans wasted no time in inviting them to dinner at the local Hotel Lion D'Or. The mixed "binge" went off splendidly, punctuated now and then by a flying plate or a zooming saucer, much to the handwringing distress of the waiters and management. Before the party adjourned there wasn't anything that was throwable still intact. That was a Limey version of "Let us celebrate and you pay the breakage, Yank." All hands, though, considered it a smashing good party, shattered crockery, black eyes and all. There were Canucks, there were Aussies and a sprinkling of Anzacs.

The opportunity to repay them was forthcoming the next day. An invitation from the British commanding officer asking the Americans to mess that evening was promptly accepted.

"Now, my boys," said Lufbery with a mischievous gleam in his eye, "here is where we even the score with the Limeys. You, Bert,

U. S. Signal Corps

Same man, different uniform: Raoul Lufbery (left) after he joined the U. S. Air Service.

James Norman Hall (right), a comrade of Raoul Lufbery's in the Lafayette Escadrille who transferred with him to the U.S.A.S., flying with the 94th. Hall had a remarkable career, was probably the only pilot in the war who served under three flags. He went out in 1914 with the British infantry, was wounded and discharged, enlisted again in the French service and transferred to the Lafayette Escadrille, then transferred to the U.S.A.S. He was shot down behind German lines while flying with the 94th and ended the war as a prisoner. With Charles Nordhoff he wrote the well known two-volume WWI history of the Lafayette Escadrille.

*Quoted by permission from One Man's War by Bert Hall. G. P. Putnam & Sons, N.Y.C., 1929

ACE OF THE LAFAYETTE

Kiffin, Nimmie and Bill, don't fail me tonight. When I holler out 'scramble,' put both shoulders into it..."

The war was temporarily suspended again, as the rafters rang to toasts to King George V, to President Poincaré and to Woodrow Wilson. Lufbery, sharp eyed as a hungry fox on the prowl, was watching everyone. The hosts, aware the Yanks were going to do wrong by them, just didn't know when or where. They figured the quality as well as the massive quantity of the drinks would slow down the avengers. Suddenly, like a typhoon, the signal came. The resulting carnage smashed every chair, table, dish and bottle. Flimsy little partitions that divided the room simply melted before the football tactics of the Americans. The Britishers didn't seem to mind at all. Over in one corner Captain Thenault and the British major were drinking each other's health between explosions of laughter, as the room came tumbling down around their ears.

A burst of pistol shots outside punctuated the merriment and brought a momentary halt to the bacchanalian destruction. "What the bloody, bloomin' hell was that?" exclaimed the major.

Looking out the window, the celebrants beheld an astonishing scene. A tall Canuck was shooting at a book held at arm's length by none other than the ringleader of the brawl. "Come on, hit it again," yelled Lufbery. The Canuck was a crack shot, too, for in spite of the wavering target offered by Lufbery he was hitting the book every shot. When at last the escadrille started home, the Royal Naval Air Service officers voiced the unanimous opinion that they were the best gang of Yanks they'd ever encountered.

"We didn't expect you bloody blighters would be 'arf so sociable, you know," said one pilot. "Not 'arf."

One day Hall and Lufbery went out on patrol and got separated. When Luf got home his Nieuport was a complete wreck, fit only for the junk pile, and his helmet was perforated by a bullet hole.

"What the hell happened to you?" Hall asked.

National Archives

Lufbery swore long and vehemently. "Bertie, it would take two Philadelphia lawyers and a Boston solicitor to tell how that fight came out. All I know is that I couldn't see you, and as I was quietly shooting one Heinie's tail full of lead, forty of the buggers hopped me. I pulled in my ears and hopped for home. Look at the wreck of that old Nieuport and you'll know the answer to all such damn fool questions!"

On another occasion Hall and Lufbery got parted in the midst of a bullet-punctuated melee and this time Hall was the straggler. When he landed, Lufbery was waiting to hear his side of the scrap.

"I thought I was a goner." Hall related. "His bursts cut through my top wing and struts just like a scythe. I'd gotten in some bursts myself at close range so when the flames burst out of his cockpit I knew it was all over. The confirmation was a cinch."

"Afire, Bertie?" Luf asked.

"Yes, Luf. Over Fort Douaumont."

"God, it's awful to burn up in the air. I'll never do it. I'll go over the side before I get cremated. Me for jumping."

Lufbery was a terrific ladies' man, and the stench of cheap perfume permeated his billets. Every *fille de joie* in Paris wrote him, and he spent hours answering them in longhand. His squadron mates, including famed Hollywood dance director LeRoy Prinz, thought he was writing his memoirs. To their great disappointment they discovered his experiences were not being saved for posterity but only for his current girl friends.

As the tempo of the second battle of Verdun slackened and the French knew they would hold their lines, rumors started circulating through the hangars of the escadrille. There was talk of a new front, perhaps Gallipoli. Finally the news was official. The escadrille was to pack its personal equipment, move up to Le Bourget, get new planes and fly to a new sector.

With nostalgic sadness, Lufbery, Kiffen Rockwell and Bert Hall taxied their battered Nieuports out on the tarmac for the last time. Captain Thenault banged out a tune on the piano, then gathered up his police dog mascot, "Fram." The train ride to Paris turned into an all day picnic as the surviving members of the escadrille, singing and whistling away their regrets, tried to forget the missing faces—Victor Chapman, Clyde Balsley, Jim McConnell, Elliot Cowdin, Dennis Dowd, Jimmy Bach, Eugene Bertin.

They hadn't been in Paris two hours until one of the lads spotted an advertisement in a newspaper.

"Hey, guys, look at this! Woman wants to sell a lion cub. Let's buy it for the squadron as a good luck mascot."

"For the luvva Pete," derided Lufbery, "grow up. Don't be an ass all your life. What in hell would we do with a lion cub?"

"A lion is lucky and we can get this one cheap. If you won't go with me, I'll bring it back myself."

Since no argument to the contrary would prevail, the doughty pilots, getting more imbued with the holiday spirit as they progressed from one bistro to another, chartered

National Archives

ACE OF THE LAFAYETTE

a cab and drove out to a suburb of Paris. It was a doctor's wife who had advertised the beast for sale. He'd been born on board ship, and his mother was destined for a zoo in Cherbourg. Five hundred francs changed hands, and the Lafayette Escadrille now possessed a cute, bright eyed baby who tried to live up to his heritage as king of beasts by roaring in a ferocious manner. Promptly named Whiskey, he went everywhere with his masters, to bars, sidewalk cafés and in taxis.

He romped with the pilots like a big, amiable dog. For a long time dogs were his constant companions, and Lufbery claimed that was why Whiskey was so gentle, ". . . because he didn't know he was a lion and thought he was a dog." His chief pal for a year was Carranza, a nondescript hound of dubious ancestry owned by Didier Masson.

When Whiskey was a year old, they decided it was time he had a wife. After a diligent search they found a little female cub who was tagged, quite appropriately, Soda. The two got along famously, but Soda, who had a mean disposition, never became the squadron pet her mate was, being more inclined to claw and scratch. Whiskey became very attached to Lufbery and followed him around with dog-like devotion, probably attracted by the cheap toilet water Luf used. Raoul would only have to call out "Whiskey!" to have the big lion wreck everything in sight to come bounding after him. Lufbery taught the mascot a trick that eased the tension of the war with many a sidesplitting guffaw. Edwin C. Parsons, in his memoirs, described the stunt.

Visitors, mostly poilus from nearby rest camps curious to see the American flyers and their machines, came to the escadrille, skeptical of the tales of a menagerie of pet lions. Luf would wait for a good opportunity, then send the lion around the corner of the barracks out of sight while the escadrille lined up to see the fun.

His mind on other matters, the unsuspecting French doughboy would stroll down the path. Lufbery would give the signal and Whiskey, with a deep growl, would leap out, throw his huge paws over the shoulders of his victim and drag him to the ground by sheer weight. The unfortunate victim would be so petrified at the apparition of this savage beast springing out on him from nowhere that his knees would melt and he'd go down, expecting to be torn to bits.

Then Whiskey would put his head back, open his mouth, and bare all his yellowed fangs in a silent laugh. Lufbery said it was a

National Archives

Star Pupils: The five pilots at left were pupils of Raoul Lufbery while he was coaching members of the 94th Squadron in combat tactics. From left to right they are Lt. Joe Eastman, Capt. Jim Meissner (eight victories), Capt. Eddie Rickenbacker (26 victories), Capt. Reid Chambers (seven victories), Lt. Thorne Taylor (two victories). Note the insigne of the 94th Squadron (center), the famous hat-in-the-ring.

Maj. Jean Huffer (left) and Maj. Raoul Lufbery (right). Huffer, also a veteran of the French Air Service, was commander of the 94th Aero Squadron, U.S.A.S., and Lufbery, leading American ace with 17 victories, was acting as advisor and coach to Squadron 94's pilots.

laugh, although Parsons claimed Whiskey was just airing his mouth after a taste of unwashed poilu. Lufbery would then whistle and the lion would come over, purring like a big kitten. A tame lion was completely incomprehensible to the frightened soldier, too grateful at escaping a horrible death to be angry.

By June 1917 Lufbery was promoted to second lieutenant. He not only was the biggest hero in the escadrille, but a front page news item in the United States. Ten palms adorned his *Croix de Guerre* and he was named a *Chevalier* in the *Légion d'Honneur*. As that year ended and aerial warfare whipped up towards the decisive spring campaigns of 1918, attrition had laid a heavy hand on the Lafayette Escadrille. Only Bert Hall and Bill Thaw were left from the original group. Chapman, Rockwell, De Laage de Meux, McConnell and Prince were dead; Balsley had been eliminated with a nasty stomach wound in his first combat. Daring Didier Masson was off the flying roster, and Paul Pavelka had transferred to ground forces. Raw, unblooded recruits were filling the ranks.

Lufbery, tired and ailing from rheumatism which often sent him to sick bay, weary from two years of bloodletting, was not at all enthusiastic over the recruits or about anything for that matter. Sitting at Henry's Bar after dinner one night, Hall and Lufbery talked about the old days, about Bar-le-Duc and Luxeuil, about the deaths of Victor Chapman, Nimmie Prince and Kiffin Rockwell. At Hall's mention of his girl at Bourges, Lufbery shook his head sadly and in his clipped manner stated: "Pneumonia, She died last December."

Early in December of 1917 the escadrille was transferred to La Noblette on the Champagne sector. Acting on advice from higher echelons, the pilots all put in for release from the French army expecting to be immediately commissioned in the U. S. Army. They were released, but in the traditional military snafu, no commissions arrived. So until February 18, 1918 they flew as civilians in the uniform of the French Army.

The Lafayette Escadrille ceased to exist as a unit on February 18, and lock, stock and barrel became the 103rd Pursuit Squadron of the American Air Service. They were allowed to keep their Spads and Indian head insignia, but the new brass hats, eager for spit and polish discipline, refused to let them keep Whiskey and Soda. The lads parted with their mascots with moist eyes and heavy hearts. The two lions were summarily hauled off to the Paris Zoo where they soon died protesting the curtailment of their liberty. Prominent in the stone memorial to the Lafayette Escadrille in Paris are the two playful lion mascots.

Commissions finally arrived with Luf and Bill Thaw being made majors. The rest of the escadrille, their hopes of flying as a unit thwarted by higher authority, were scattered with many of them sent to Paris where they waited months for another chance to fly. Lufbery was given a shiny new desk at Issoudun, a drawer full of freshly sharpened pencils and

The gay Spad: The Germans had no monopoly on gaily decorated planes. This Spad of the 94th Aero Squadron was in good circus tradition.

absolutely nothing to do. He was too valuable now, with 17 confirmed victories, to be risked in combat. But he thoroughly hated paper work, and to be grounded like a Kiwi was heartbreaking. He fumed and fussed so loudly that finally orders came transferring him to training duties with the 94th and 95th pursuit squadrons at Villenue.

Hard luck still dogged his footsteps. The squadrons started out with a few old Nieuport 28s sans guns. So, for a month, Luf taught his fledglings combat tactics and flew them to enemy lines where they could see enemy patrols they could not attack. At last the guns came, and the 94th started patrol duty in the Toul sector. But there was little activity for the Germans were conserving every plane and pilot for the big spring *Putsch* that would make or break them. Lufbery led his daily patrols and tried his old lone eagle tactics, but to no avail. It was virtually impossible to find an enemy and harder still to force a combat.

Lufbery took an immediate liking to one of the new pilots assigned to the 94th, Eddie Rickenbacker. Rick, who had won fame as a race track driver before joining the army, soon struck up an enduring friendship with Lufbery. They talked the same language. Luf had been a dirt track driver in France before he met Marc Pourpe, had bummed around like Eddie, and had learned his lessons in the school of hard knocks rather than in a university. Lufbery often professed to envy his students. "They have youth, guts, luck and new equipment, besides being cocky," he said.

U. S. Air Force

RAOUL LUFBERY

In his memoirs, *Fighting the Flying Circus*, Rick related his first patrol over enemy lines with Luf. "Lufbery looked us over without saying much. 'Rick, you and Campbell be ready to leave at 8:15.'" Rickenbacker tried to be nonchalant as he answered "Yes sir."

The next morning Luf found the fledglings ready. He gave a few instructions to Campbell, and then cautioned Rick to keep close to him and not to break formation.

Soon the beautiful ruins of Rheims spread beneath their wings, and Rick cast one longing glance back at their field as they neared enemy lines. It seemed to Rick that Lufbery, his only salvation in this alien sky, was at least a mile ahead of him. Suddenly he made a *virage* and took up a position a few hundred feet from Rick, as though to say, "Don't worry, boy, I have an eye on you." When Archy shells started bursting around them, Rickenbacker confesses how enraged he was at the old pilots at home base who pretended to like Archy and who joked about how much it cost the Kaiser when they just cruised around and taunted the AA batteries into firing at them. (Archy was 18 pounds of shrapnel and cost $10 per load.) On that flight, Rick said, no enemy airplanes dared venture into their vicinity. On landing at home base, Lufbery, in his quiet, droll manner, asked the two rookies what they had observed on their first cruise over enemy lines. "Not another plane in the sky," they chorused.

"Just what I expected. These rookies— they're all the same. Reminds me of the three little monkeys, See No Evil, Hear No Evil, Speak No Evil." Angrily, Campbell and Rick asked him just exactly what he meant.

"Well," chuckled Lufbery, "one formation of five Spads passed under us before we crossed the lines, and another flight of five Spads went by about fifteen minutes later, and you didn't see them although they weren't five hundred yards away. It was just as well they weren't Boches. Then there were two German Albatroses two miles ahead of us when we turned back, and there was another enemy two-seater nearer us than that at about five thousand. You ought to look about a bit when you get over enemy lines. It might save your hides some day."

On May 1, 1918 Lufbery and Rickenbacker cruised over Montsec for an hour trying to spot a Hun. Then as Lufbery started for home in the direction of Pont-à-Mousson, he went into a steep dive. Rick followed, thinking he had spotted a victim. The reason for the abrupt maneuver soon became apparent. Raoul was in trouble. His prop had stopped spinning and he was looking for a landing spot. His Nieuport dropped gently down in a muddy pasture. It rolled a few feet, then nosed over. Its tail section pointed heavenward for a moment, then it gently turned over on its back flipping a cursing Lufbery out into a pile of cow dung and mud.

When a staff car retrieved him, he was none the worse except for a scratched nose and

U. S. Signal Corps

"Quirk" of the 94th: "Quirk" was British slang for an unskilled student. The pilot of this Nieuport came home upside down. It sometimes happened and usually, as in this case, the pilot just got up and walked away.

The German that got Lufbery was an Albatros C-3 gunner. This sturdy old workhorse of the Imperial Air Force had a long career (see right photo).

injured dignity. He'd blown a cylinder and had just enough altitude to glide down over Allied lines.

On May 7 the 94th suffered a stunning loss. James Norman Hall, idol of the old escadrille and most popular pilot in the new American unit, crashed and was taken prisoner. He had been out on dawn patrol that morning with Rick and Eddie Green when he shed a wing by diving his Nieuport too fast. He tried frantically to glide back to the Allied side on half power, but his engine coughed, stalled and then conked out completely. Out of control, he crashed in a pasture near Montsec and suffered a badly fractured ankle. That was the end of a glorious fighting career, and he was destined to spend the rest of the war as a prize captive in a German prison camp. Every pilot in the 94th burned to avenge the loss of their comrade.

Ten minutes after Rickenbacker and Green landed with the sad news, Lufbery was walking towards the hangar with a look of grim hatred. "Get my plane ready," he barked at his crew chief. An intimate of Hall's from old days in the escadrille, Luf was going to avenge his pal, just like he had sworn to avenge his mentor and patron, Marc Pourpe. His mechanics, noting his grim demeanor, had his plane out and were loading gas and checking ammo belts. One of them handed Raoul his helmet, and without saying a word, he climbed into his "office," gunned the motor and headed straight for the enemy lines.

He cruised for over an hour without meeting an enemy plane of any description. Then with barely a half hour's supply of petrol in his tank, he flew deep over German lines to tackle singlehanded three Fokkers he'd spotted north of St. Mihiel. One fighter fell in flames before his short, savage bursts, and the other two broke and ran for home. An advance observation post confirmed this victory the next day, and his victory parade now stood at 18 enemy planes. He probably had closer to 40 planes counting those that were too far back of enemy lines to be officially confirmed. He was America's top ace, his name on every tongue in the States. He was a colorful, gallant D'Artagnan, a flaming cavalier of the skies. He had more than avenged the untimely end of Marc Pourpe, and in some measure had evened the score on Jimmy Hall.

This was Lufbery's last victory, for the sands of time were running out. Sunday, May 19, was a balmy, spring day, and the war seemed like only a distant cloud on the horizon. Suddenly cannon shots shattered the quiet Sabbath morning. The antiaircraft guns atop St. Mihiel began to belch puff-balls of high smoke. A telephonic alert— radios and control towers were almost unknown in World War I—informed the 94th that a German photographic reconnaissance plane was due over Nancy momentarily. There were always planes on the tarmac alerted for an emergency like this. At that fateful moment the only pilot ready to go

Smithsonian Institution

was youthful, inexperienced Lieutenant Gude, new to combat. Just as he got airborne, the French AA batteries stilled their fire, certain they had clobbered the intruder. Sure enough, the Hun plane began spinning in, but at 200 feet it leveled out and started to head for German lines. Eager to make a good showing over his home field, Gude got trigger happy and wasted his ammo at an impossible range without scoring any damage.

Hollywood director LeRoy Prinz, a first lieutenant in the 94th, was a spectator at this last and tragic chapter in Lufbery's life. Luf had been watching the futile effort of Gude to bring down the German plane. When he saw the German escaping, he vaulted onto a motorcycle and rushed to the tarmac. His own plane was out of commission, so he grabbed the nearest plane, one belonging to Davis. The mechanics assured him that the craft was ready, so without further ado Lufbery gunned the Nieuport off the field and started in pursuit. It was typical of Lufbery, this impulsive dash to clobber the invader, but this time the deck was stacked against him. With all of his long string of victories, he had never brought down a plane over Allied lines, and the chance to get one over his home field could not be passed. So he gambled on an unfamiliar ship, one whose guns certainly were not as precisely aligned as his own.

Prinz relates a graphic account of this last fight of Lufbery's: "Within five minutes Luf was in range of the high flying Hun and fired several short bursts as he closed in. Then he veered away, apparently to clear a jammed gun. He zeroed in at point-blank range and fired several long bursts with absolutely no effect. Why, hell, he might as well have been firing feathers instead of bullets. We found out why later. The two-seater Albatros was armor plated.

"Suddenly Raoul Lufbery's Nieuport 28 wobbled and tossed like a stick in a windstorm. A great ball of crimson flame fanned out from the cockpit. The agonized cry came from a hundred throats simultaneously, 'He's on fire!'"

Lufbery's luck had indeed run out. The Nieuport 28 had a gas tank on the right side next to the pilot, and the wily Boche gunner had punctured this vulnerable spot with a burst of tracers. Lufbery made frantic efforts to sideslip the tiny ship and blow the flames away from his body. But within seconds the Nieuport was a roaring inferno. Unable to stand the searing flames, and true to his statements to Bert Hall and Ed Parsons that "If I get aflame, I'll jump. I'm not going to roast alive," Lufbery climbed out on the left wing.

He jumped, trying to aim himself like a projectile, on the million-to-one chance he could hit the Toul Canal hundreds of feet below. It was a futile hope, for he smashed onto a white picket fence that bordered a small cottage in the quaint village of Maron, just north of Nancy. He gasped out his last few precious moments of life cradled in the arms of a peasant woman.

The ill-omened Nieuport flew on a few miles, the flames that drove Lufbery over the side now extinguished. Then it crashed and burned, in complete and final destruction. It was ironic that German flyers were saving themselves with crude parachutes, while Allied flyers who had no such device either had to crash and burn to death in their flaming coffins or put a bullet in their heads with the .45 caliber automatics they carried. Some, like Lufbery, preferred to jump overboard when the luck ran out.

When Prinz, Rickenbacker and the others reached the scene, they found that the townspeople had removed the charred body to the town hall and had gently covered it with a great mound of fragrant flowers from their gardens.

In an epilogue to the downing of Lufbery, the Albatros was later shot down, but not before it marked up another casualty, a French ace who pursued the Hun after Lufbery crashed. Inspection of the wreckage of the German ship showed that Lufbery had been pumping his bullets into armor plate.

Thus ended the odyssey of Raoul Lufbery. The wheel of fortune had spun full circle and the restless journey was ended. Born in France, he returned there to find his destiny, to die a hero's death, fighting to the very last. Almost two years to the day after he joined the Lafayette Escadrille, he was laid to rest in the soil of his native country with every honor a sorrowful France and America could bestow. •

Edward Mannock
The Crippled Eagle

By William E. Barrett

O N APRIL 1, 1915 a tall, lean, angry Irishman named Edward Mannock was released from a Turkish prison camp. He had been interned as a British subject when Turkey became the ally of Germany in World War I. Now Turkey was sending him home, released because of "age, bad health and defective eyesight."

The release was more humiliating than the captivity because it dismissed Edward Mannock as unimportant, such a poor physical specimen that he would never be a menace to the Central Powers. Mannock, who feared that the Turks were correct and that he would never be able to strike back, cursed his captors. He was always to hate bitterly all Germans, all Turks—and war. They had cost him much.

At the time Edward Mannock was 30 years old. He had climbed a long way before the quarrels of nations cut the ground from under him. He was the son of a man who spent a lifetime in the British Army without rising above the rank of corporal, a selfish, brutal, hard-drinking man who deserted his family when Edward was 12 years old. There were brothers and sisters and a frail mother in that deserted household and Edward Mannock had to get what education he could while working at any job that he could find.

His neighbors remembered him long years afterwards as a thin, eager, cheerful youngster who was forever looking for work and who

EDWARD MANNOCK

never complained about any job that he found, no matter how difficult. The saving gift for that small boy was that everything interested him—everything that grew, every piece of machinery that moved, everything that men did for a living and every word that was ever printed.

His left eye was curiously contracted, a congenital defect, and he covered it with his hand when he read, but the weakness did not discourage him from reading. He particularly loved poetry and memorized long passages from the major poets. When he was still very young he developed a love for Shakespeare which he never lost. His vocabulary was large and he spoke with a strange eloquence. A neighbor, who admired him and could not pay him money for odd jobs, gave him music lessons. He sold papers and carried messages and worked as a porter in a barber shop among many other jobs. He sang on street corners for pennies.

In the years of his growing up, no one called Mannock "Edward." He attracted nicknames wherever he went. For many years he was called "Pat," then "Murph." He had the gift of making friends and was a good companion with a natural Irish wit. His family responsibilities followed him into his twenties and absorbed the little money he earned, but he had a driving ambition to "amount to something," to prove that he was "as good as any other man." The caste system of England kept the badly educated son of a noncommissioned army man in humble jobs but this did not discourage him.

Mannock joined the Socialist Party in his twenties and through his experience at meetings became an eloquent speaker. He believed sincerely in the principles of socialism which seemed to hold the only practical answer to the poverty and injustice which he saw all around him. He wanted to change the hard conditions of life for others through political action and, to accomplish this, he worked to change his own life through study, patience and initiative.

He was working as a lineman for the telephone company and studying telephone engineering through a correspondence course when he read an ad in the paper. The British-controlled telephone company of Constantinople needed an engineer. Mannock had no chance with his slight qualifications if he applied by mail, so he resigned his job, shipped as a crew member on a tramp steamer and went to Turkey. That was January 1914.

With his charm, eloquence and gift of bluff, he not only talked his way into the job that he wanted but did so well as an engineer that he was promoted within six months. In November Turkey entered the war against England and his career was over. He had achieved a solid position among people better educated than he, and he had achieved it by patient study and hard work. At 30 the coming of war stripped him of his achievement and of his dreams.

That war, in Mannock's mind, was a German war. No one will ever understand Mannock who does not understand that.

There was only one role in the war for an "unfit" man like Mannock—the Home Guard. It consisted of old men, crippled men, men of limited usefulness. The proud, hotheaded Mannock could not stand the feeling of inferiority that it forced on him. He went back to the grim business of studying alone, of bluffing, of building himself up "as good

Maj. Edward (Micky) Mannock, V.C., Britain's top ranking WW I ace. Mannock, a controversial figure, was almost unknown during his life.

Royal Air Force

THE CRIPPLED EAGLE

as any man." He applied for a commission in the Royal Engineers, an outfit that demanded technical knowledge rather than physical perfection. On April 1, 1916 Mannock received his commission as a second lieutenant.

During that summer of 1916 the Royal Flying Corps was capturing the public imagination. The great aerial knight was Captain Albert Ball, a youngster in his teens who had an almost miraculous flying skill and an uncanny gift with guns.

Mannock became one of Ball's hero-worshippers. "There's the man I'd like to be," he said. The idea of individual combat appealed to him, fighting the war man to man. It seemed a hopeless dream for a man over 30 with only one good eye, but Mannock's life would have been hopeless from the beginning if he had ever surrendered to odds.

An officer from any branch had the privilege of applying for a transfer to the Royal Flying Corps and age limits were often waived for men of technical knowledge. But Mannock's commanding officer took a dim view of his ambition and tried to discourage him.

"Tut, tut, my lad," he said. "We do a good job. This flying is romantic nonsense."

Mannock was stubbornly insistent. "You won't stand in my way?" he asked.

"No. I won't do that. But the medicos will. You haven't got the eyes for it, lad."

Mannock knew that he didn't have the eyes. He did have guile and charm and a stage magician's gift for distracting attention—and he had an incredible memory. Through some means known only to himself, he got hold of a set of eye charts used by the R.F.C. doctors and memorized them. He succeeded in bluffing his way past the doctors and was accepted for training by the R.F.C. in August 1916 and assigned to the school of military aeronautics at Reading.

The planes at Reading were old pusher biplanes and the students were fatalistic youngsters who accepted cheerfully the fact that the flying schools would kill more of them than the Germans would. It was the year of the R.F.C. song:

> *Stand to your glasses steady*
> *This world is a world of lies*
> *So, here's to the dead already*
> *And hurrah for the next man*
>   *who dies.*

Mannock got along better with the ships than with the students. He had good hands, an understanding of combustion engines and a feeling that the air was his element. He learned to handle a plane in the air with astonishing ease, but he baffled his instructor by losing all of his skill when he came in for a landing. That was Mannock's personal problem and he could not confide it to anyone. He discovered the hard way why the R.F.C. demanded 20-20 vision of pilots. There was, for one thing, the matter of depth perception. He did not see anything in depth as it actually was. He had to land on an airdrome that wasn't where his one good eye told him it was. Invariably he leveled off high, running his wheels on a strip that wasn't there.

Other students had normal problems and they took them lightheartedly. When the strain of the day was over, they drank and

Mannock's instructor and friend, Maj. James Byford (Jimmy) McCudden, V.C., held every rank in the R.F.C. and R.A.F. from private to major and was officially credited with 57 victories. He was killed in an accident while he was taking off in his S.E. 5a on July 9, 1918.

Central News

rioted and sang. Mannock, ten or a dozen years older than most of them, had the example of his father before him and he did not drink. He was concentrating upon finding an answer to his problem of landings and the only time he participated in the social life of the mess was when a political, social or religious argument started. At such times he out-talked everyone else with the fire and conviction of a man who signed his letters to his friends "Socialistically yours." Young flying students, with no strong convictions of any kind, walked wide of him.

"A rum type," they decided. "A solemn soul!"

They called him "The Mick" and it was a nickname that Mannock resented. He sensed derision in it, the scorn of educated young Englishmen for a rough, self-educated Irishman. It angered him more than he would have been angered by a blow and through most of his service with the R.F.C. he was on guard with new people he met, expecting to be patronized and prepared to resent it. Oddly enough the derisive "Mick" became ultimately the friendly appellation "Micky" and that was the last nickname that Mannock bore, the one that endured. He learned to like being called "Mick", too. It had friendliness and affection in it if no one put "the" before it.

Despite the bad landings which he improved only slightly by concentration, Mannock moved on to advance flight training at Joyce Green and into the hands of the man who saved his flying career. His new instructor was a handsome, cocky, assured young man, a glittering ace on leave from the front, easy, affable, impatient with lazy students but attracted to serious ones. This was the great James Byford (Jimmy) McCudden who had gone out with one of the first four R.F.C. Squadrons in 1914. Mannock was awed by him and McCudden, who did not consider any student introduced until he tried him in the air, seemed indifferent.

The two men went aloft together in an old Vickers Gunbus, a two-seater pusher with a bathtub nacelle which held two men with the prop and the engine behind them and clear

S.E. 5 in flight: The S.E. was one of the greatest fighting planes of the war, and was the favorite of many of the British aces. Mannock flew the ship with 74 Squadron, and the flight he commanded scored 70 victories in two months. American pilots with the British also flew this ship.

R. R. Martin

vision ahead. McCudden, a master of acrobatics, put the clumsy looking ship through loops, spins, dives and Immelmanns without disconcerting his pupil who did the same maneuvers confidently when he was given the controls. McCudden slapped Mannock on the shoulder after they landed.

"You'll do, Old Son," he said. "I want to talk to you."

That was in February 1917. Jimmy McCudden was not quite 22 and Mannock was 31, but McCudden was the senior, the man of experience in the thing that Mannock wanted to do. McCudden talked to him. They were men of similar backgrounds. McCudden, too, was of Irish blood, the son of a noncommissioned officer with limited education; but he carried no chip on his shoulder.

"It makes no difference who you are in the R.F.C.," he said, "but you'll meet some snobs. The squadron mess is your club and you belong to it. Nothing else matters."

He spent a lot of time with Mannock. He instructed him dual, then had him go up alone while he flew another ship in mock combat with him, teaching him the tricks. He spent time with him on the ground discussing his theories of combat and there was, in all the war years, no more thoughtful student of aerial tactics than Jimmy McCudden.

When Mannock graduated and received his orders to the 40th Squadron in France, a Nieuport scout squadron, Ball was still his idol but McCudden was his friend. He had absorbed into himself more of McCudden than he realized.

Mannock landed at Boulogne en route to his squadron on April 1, 1917. For the third year in a row the first of April was a significant date in his life and he accepted it as a good omen.

A pilot in the R.F.C. needed all of the good omens he could find in April 1917. The British were preparing for the big push which was scheduled to get off on Easter Monday, April 9. It was the job of the old, slow, outmoded two-seaters to fly behind the German lines all day taking pictures and spotting targets for the British guns, scurrying out in the early morning to note the results of the night's bombardment. It was the job of the scouts, the pursuit squadrons, to protect the two-seaters when they could but, at all costs, to prevent German observation planes from obtaining an accurate picture of British preparations and concentrations of troops.

The British pilots flew to their many jobs in the ships of 1916 and against them the German concentrated new, fast models of greater speed and maneuverability. The British, to obtain the necessary front fire for pursuit pilots, gave them pushers like the D.H.2 with the gun mounted on the nose of the nacelle, or tractors like the French Nieuport 27 with a Lewis gun mounted on the top center section to fire over the prop.

The Germans had machine guns synchronized to fire through the propeller and their best scout, the Albatros D-2, had twin machine guns so synchronized. Against these odds, committed to a task beyond their numbers, the R.F.C. losses were staggering.

The guns were blazing all along the front. It was dark and raining when Mannock arrived at Squadron 40's headquarters. He had been under fire for the first time en route and his nerves were jumpy but he was excited too. He braced himself to meet new people, always a difficult task for him. Meeting his fellow pilots for the first time, he seated himself at the table in the mess with a joking remark. No one laughed. One tight-lipped pilot said "That's Pell's chair you're sitting in. He didn't come back today."

Mannock covered his own confusion with belligerence. "If he was still sitting in it, I wouldn't be here," he said. "I've come to do a job."

It was an unfortunate remark and the other pilots remembered it later. Captain Todd of C flight to whom Mannock was assigned was not affected by quick tempers or hasty judgments in the mess. Veterans of Squadron 40 were being killed every day and he did not risk a new man over the lines until he was broken in. He took Mannock out at dawn and flew with him behind the British lines to initiate him into front line flying. "Stay on your own side for a few days," he said, "and get the feel of it."

Mannock was impatient to fight, but he discovered in the relatively safe area over which he flew that this was not like flying in England. The Battle of Arras was in full swing and the roads were choked with transport. The bombardment was incessant and he had no safe landmarks to help his faulty vision. Everything on the ground that could be camouflaged was camouflaged.

He had his old trouble with landings and he cracked up two ships badly in his first two days. With Nieuports scarce at the front that was an unpardonable sin. Other men landed their ships after being badly shot up, had them patched and flew back to battle while a clumsy tyro destroyed perfectly sound ships. Mannock had to go to St. Omer for a new ship and weather delayed his return for several days. C flight, flying one man short, cursed him.

A grim Mannock welcomed his first patrol over the lines on April 13. It had snowed during the night and the morning was gray, windy and wet. He flew into German aerial territory behind Captain Todd and suddenly the sky around him seemed to explode. Great black bursts of smoke, red-hearted bursts, surrounded him and the sound was like a loud clapping. He had a hard time controlling his plane in the zigzag avoidance maneuver. This was "Archy"—antiaircraft fire. It absorbed his attention for several minutes and in those few minutes he lost his flight. They vanished somewhere in the murky sky and Mannock had to fly home alone. He did the same thing on his next patrol and Captain Todd heard his explanation and shook his head doubtfully.

"It isn't done, Mannock," he said. "You must stay close to me and watch my signals."

Mannock was experiencing panic. He had tried to fly close and he had been aware of the signals as the flight changed altitude and direction constantly, but he could not see the Germans whom the others obviously saw and he did not know what the flight was doing, or why. His eye was not trained to these conditions. Unless he could see, he could not fight.

When he wasn't assigned to patrol, Mannock spent hours in the air alone, diving at the ground targets to test his guns, then landing to adjust the gun sights. He had to fashion a gun sight for a one-eyed man and he had to do it himself. Some of the other pilots said that it was much safer to shoot at targets than at Huns.

They also said that the F.E.8 which they had before they got Nieuports had been a better ship. They did not trust the frail Nieuport wings in a dive. "No one can known when they will pull off, or how," one pilot said.

"We could find out," Mannock told him.

The next morning Mannock went up and dived his Nieuport at the drome. He came down almost to the carpet with the high

United Artists

Combat shot? This is strictly from Hollywood, a movie combat photographed for the film, *Hell's Angels*. It purports to show S.E. 5s fighting Fokker D-7s. One error is the fact that the Fokker D-7s never flew with the old Maltese Cross insigne.

scream of the wires in his ears, adjusting mentally for the deceit of his one eye, almost skimming the drome and zooming back to repeat the performance. He dived for long distances and he steepened his dive each time he came down until, at last, a strut broke and the right lower wing came off. Mannock righted his crippled ship, cleared the squadron hangar by inches and came down in a ploughed field. The plane flipped over on its back but Mannock was unhurt.

He swaggered a little as he walked away. Nieuport wings would take a lot of punishment and he had proved it.

He did not swagger long. On his next patrol, C flight dived on two German observation planes and Mannock had his first taste of combat. Here were the Germans; two clumsy, wide-winged, black-crossed ships. He saw a tense German airman behind his guns in a rear cockpit. Mannock had dreamed of this moment and when it came it was horror. There were four of his own ships and two Germans in one hazed blur of action. His eye could not adjust to the speed and the swift whirling flight of two Nieuports diving under the Germans, two sweeping over them. He pulled out, dived away and went home.

He reported that his guns had jammed but no one believed him. He could not tell them the truth. None of those ships had been where his eye said they were. He had almost collided with another plane of the flight which had seemed a safe distance away when actually he was right on top of it.

He should, perhaps, have told the truth then, given up flying and returned to England. It never occurred to him.

He pulled out of another fight the next day. The enemy was again only awkward, helpless two-seaters which were outnumbered by the English; not fast, flashy German scouts which would have had the advantage of numbers, horsepower and armament. This time Mannock claimed engine trouble and no one spoke to him. He was classified definitely now as a coward.

The outward character of Mannock was changing. He was in a desperate situation and he kept assuring himself that he could learn to see truly in combat, could train his eye if only he had time. Time was rushing past in a month of terrific R.F.C. casualties. He knew how his conduct appeared to others. He could not answer or explain. He could only fly out for hours at a time alone, the solo flights that other pilots labeled "Hun avoidance," practicing landings on clouds, flying low around church steeples and other obstacles; training his vision to the proper proportion between what his eye reported and what actually existed in terms of distance and depth. At the end of the day he fought the Battle of the Mess.

Most wartime pilots drank a lot when the day's duty in the air ended. They drank to relax, to let the tension run out of their nerves, to forget the killing that they had done and the comrades they had lost. Micky Mannock, who had always avoided liquor, lived with more tension, frustration and fear than anyone in the squadron and, unable to confide in anyone, needed companionship. He learned to drink in 40 Squadron and he was not accustomed to it. His natural love of argument was intensified by liquor, as was his hatred of the Germans; so he talked too much and tried too hard to convince other men that he was the equal of anybody. He thrust himself upon men who did not respect or like him, and they considered him a bore. When all else failed, he sought to impress them with his toughness. He wanted to box or wrestle. De Burgh, one of the veteran pilots who was a burly athlete and fond of arguments himself, was the only one who would accommodate him. The two men slammed each other all around the squadron hut and the other pilots considered it "a pretty rum show."

On the same front in 60 Squadron, a young Canadian named Bishop, who came up to the front only one week before Mannock did, scored 12 victories in that month of April, was promoted to Captain and awarded the M.C. In the mess of 40 Squadron, Bishop's exploits were fully discussed and pointed regret was expressed that he had not been assigned to Squadron 40.

Mannock's record for April 1917, Bloody April when Squadron 40 lost half its strength in desperate aerial warfare, was written on the squadron log in one damning line—"Mannock—40 hours patrol over the lines—no combats."

He didn't have a single bullet hole in his wings as a souvenir of that terrible month and during the first days of May he touched rock bottom. A pilot could fall no lower.

Spring had come to France, a spring of clear, bright skies. Captain Keen, who had replaced Todd as flight leader, took Mannock out on a two-man patrol to see if he could unravel the mystery of a man who flew superbly and who would not fight. Mannock did not see the three German scouts who dived on them until Keen came around to meet them in a swift climbing turn. Caught at a disadvantage, Mannock spun out and none of the Germans followed him down. Keen, alone with three foes, shot one of them down, fought his way free of the others and flew home with his plane riddled.

"They got Mannock," he said. "I saw him go down when the fight started."

He was astonished when Mannock landed a few minutes later, still without a single bullet hole in his machine.

It was the end for Micky Mannock and he knew it. He had had no excuse and there was no doubt in his mind that he would be washed out of the squadron as soon as the commanding officer acted on Keen's report. He had one more chance to redeem himself, only one. He flew another patrol with C flight and as they crossed into German territory, Mannock took a desperate gamble to regain the respect that he had lost. He flew up beside Keen's plane, waggled his wings as a signal of his intention, and went down on a German observation balloon.

Balloons were deadly game. They were ringed with antiaircraft guns which were ranged to send up crisscross, converging fire above the big bag. Fighter pilots left them strictly alone unless specifically instructed to get them. Mannock dived straight down on top of the bag through an inferno of fire from the surprised Archy gunners. He destroyed the balloon and he got away with his gamble, but his ship was severely damaged by shrapnel which missed both the pilot and his vulnerable gasoline tank. It was Mannock's first aerial victory and there was no questioning the cold nerve that it took to get it.

Late that day, May 7, 1917, Captain Albert Ball was killed behind the German lines.

Mannock felt the shock of Ball's death keenly. Ball was his idol. Mannock had been very close to death above the balloon and he sat alone that night, facing himself. He knew with certainty, then, that he would never be like Ball, never the kind of fighting pilot that Ball was. "I have not the recklessness for it," he wrote later. "It's a different kind of a man I am. I must be as I am."

He was being discussed in the mess while he brooded alone. A new flight commander had arrived; Captain G. L. (Zulu) Lloyd, a veteran of 60 Squadron. It interested him greatly when he was told that a pilot who had gone alone that day after a balloon was classified as no good, a quitter under fire, a liar, a bluffer who let other men down to save his own skin. There was a mystery about this man Mannock that intrigued him and, after he had looked at the squadron record which seemed to confirm all that he had heard, he sat alone with Mannock and faced the issue.

"There's something the matter with you," he said. "You're not doing your job. I'm not prepared to believe what your flying mates say of you—not after that balloon show of yours—but you may be in my flight on some patrols and you've got to convince me that you belong in a fighting squadron. Now, what's the matter with you?"

It was Mannock's opportunity to explain about his defective vision, to deny the charges of cowardice which had been made against him. He considered and then he did something that called for more courage than anything he had ever done in the air. Micky Mannock, the proud, stubborn Irishman who never conceded that any man was better than himself, said humbly; "I was afraid. I believe I have conquered fear. I can do now what I couldn't do before."

"Zulu" Lloyd went to the commander and recommended that Mannock be given a leave instead of being returned to England for reclassification. That leave was the turning point of Mannock's career. He rested, and he saw air fighting and its purpose clearly as he had never seen it before.

Combat flying was unimportant. The command had more efficient metho killing men than picking them off or one in the air, and it had not created a service to provide romantic employmen young men. The value of the airplane was that it provided eyes for the guns, guiding artillery fire and registering the hits. It reached, too, where the guns did not, by dropping bombs. It brought back vital information about enemy troop movements. The ideal situation would be to have airplanes while the enemy had none, but that wasn't the way of it. So there had to be air fighters, professional killers in fast ships to knock down the enemy's useful planes.

"And that's my job," Mannock decided. "If I knock down an enemy two-seater I may save a lot of English lives on the ground. If I save one of our two-seaters from a Hun, that two-seater may cost the Germans a lot of lives."

It was all clear in his mind. Dueling was bad arithmetic. It was one German for one Englishman as the law of averages would work it out. The sane approach was to practice patience, study the enemy, always attack him at his disadvantage and avoid combat if the enemy had the advantage.

Three days after he returned to his squadron, Mannock was a changed and dedicated man. He shot down a German two-seater. He got another on the following day. He now knew how to make accurate allowances for his tricky vision and once he was confident of that, he was invincible.

His long practice with the guns was paying off and he flew volunteer patrols and solo hunting expeditions every day to test his theories about attacking enemy planes at their disadvantage. Among other feats he destroyed three balloons, attacking them scientifically by racing in low out of antiaircraft range, zooming up at them and firing his bursts, then rolling out of the ground fire and racing back the way he came. It was still risky business, but a calculated risk.

Before the month was over, Mannock was awarded the Military Cross and promoted to acting-captain in command of a flight. The poor follower became a great leader, the best flight leader, probably, of the entire war. Leadership called for planning, calculation, patience. As a commander he felt himself responsible for the life of every man he led and he had unlimited opportunity for practicing his theories of attack, watching enemy planes and flights from a distance while he maneuvered carefully to put them at the disadvantage of wind and sun before attacking.

Mannock had his own calculated techniques for attacking each type of German ship and he had studied them all. One at-

A pilot of 74 Squadron proudly posts the unit's score on June 21, 1918. The squadron was newly formed in April 1918, and Mannock joined it as a flight leader. He trained his pilots so well that they were able to score 70 victories in two months—with the loss of only one British plane and pilot. Micky Mannock himself scored a grand total of 21 victories during the same two months.

Imperial War Museum

EDWARD MANNOCK

tacked a Rumpler observation plane in a different manner than a Halberstadt which was tougher, or a Hannoveranner which could be very dangerous indeed. One did not attack German pursuit ships at all except with the advantage of surprise and superior numbers. He demonstrated his techniques of attack by going down on a solitary two-seater alone while his flight flew above him or by going down on it with a young pilot who needed experience.

Mannock's critics said that it was a cheap way of running up his personal score but he no longer paid attention to critics. He was building the most deadly flight in France and he knew what he was doing. His eye had developed an almost perfect compensation and he no longer had to make conscious corrections for what he saw. He could spot enemy formations at great distances when men with two eyes saw nothing and he could come up under an enemy ship precisely in its blind spot where it could not return his fire.

By the end of 1917 Mannock had a Bar to his Military Cross and he was credited with 20 confirmed victories, but his greatest source of pride was that as a flight leader, leading offensive and defensive patrols in all weathers, *he had not lost a man.*

Mannock was posted home for three months to train young pilots at London Colney as McCudden had trained him. He should have had the glamor of a McCudden, but he didn't have. The public knew nothing about him and, despite his great record as a flight leader, his reputation in the R.F.C. was clouded.

The pilots of 40 Squadron who knew him in his first futile months had practically all left the squadron before he returned to it; rewarded for their great work during Bloody April with flight or squadron commands, training commands or other posts. Few of them believed that the Mannock they knew had changed into a deadly fighter and they told unflattering anecdotes about him which circulated widely.

"A shifty beggar any way you took him." one famous ace said. "Couldn't even look a man in the eye."

He was right, of course. In those desperate early months, Mannock concealed his bad eye by adopting a habit of drooping his eye-

The 85th Squadron, R.A.F., on the day that Micky Mannock assumed command in June 1918. Many Americans, some of whom later achieved fame, served in this squadron which was immortalized in the great war diary, *War Birds*. Some of the familiar names from that book are: McGregor of New Zealand (second from left); Inglis who figured in Mannock's last fight (third from left); Larry Callahan of Chicago (fourth), Elliott White Springs (fifth). "Nigger" Horn has his right hand on his goggles and the police dog's paw is on his shoulder. Longton of North Dakota is standing bareheaded behind the goat. Mannock was helping Inglis score his first when he went down in flames.

Imperial War Museum

lids and he did not meet the eyes of other men. He did not pose for pictures, either, because the camera did not respect his secret.

It was April again when Mannock returned to France and the war, but 1918 was the first war year in which first of April had no significance. Nothing of importance happened to him on April 1. Mannock laughed at himself for taking that as a bad omen, "the losing of his luck," but he was sufficiently superstitious to note it and mention it to friends.

Mannock could not complain of his luck, however, on this trip to France. He went out with a new squadron, 74, with which he had been training for two months. It was composed of picked men and he was given command of flight A flying the S.E.5, considered by many the best British pursuit ship of the war. He had a Vickers gun synchronized to fire through the propeller and a Lewis gun mounted on the top center section. He was equipped, he commanded good men, men he knew, and he scored the squadron's first victory in its first day of operation, April 12, 1918.

That was the beginning of an amazing streak. Mannock picked up in 74 Squadron where he had left off in 40; training his flight to follow his lead, his philosophy of combat, his methods of attack. He worked out his methods in the laboratory of the sky with live specimens, shooting down enemy planes in precise demonstrations; training his men to be even more formidable than his famous flight in Squadron 40. Because they were picked men, he succeeded.

In two months, Mannock's flight had 70 confirmed victories, 70 German planes verified as destroyed, *with the loss of only one man.* Mannock scored 21 of those victories personally and there is evidence that he would have had many more if he had not set up kills for other pilots in his flight when they needed the morale boost of a victory. One of his flight, Lieutenant Van Ira, wrote in his diary on June 1, 1918: "Flying with Mannock is perfectly safe. His leadership is foolproof." The statistics supported that statement. The odds against any Germans opposing flight A of Squadron 74 were 70 to 1.

It was Micky Mannock's tragedy that he dimmed his own fame while he was earning it. Some very dark streaks in his nature emerged during those months of triumph and his greatest abnormality was his obsessive love of fire, of sending enemy ships down in flames.

"It's our job to destroy them," he said. "When they burn you know they're gone, and a flamer is always a confirmed victory."

Most pilots were sickened when an enemy ship burned under their guns and many of them were repelled to hear a fellow pilot gloating over the blazing deaths he caused—and Mannock did gloat. It was known that he instructed his armorer to load his guns with an exceptionally high proportion of tracer bullets, which were incendiary, but which he might have needed because of his bad vision. There was a darker rumor that he often loaded his guns with Buckingham incendiary bullets, usually reserved for balloons, when no balloon attack was planned.

Mannock certainly scored many flaming victories and he was always excited in the mess after he had burned an enemy in the air. He would graphically describe every detail. His favorite method of indicating upon his return to the field that he had scored such a victory was a circular gesture with his finger, a hissing sound with his lips, and the three words—"SIZZLE, SIZZLE, WONK!"

One English journalist, who made a special trip to 70 Squadron to write an article about the amazing Mannock, tore up his notes after hearing Mannock's enthusiastic description of a German plane, with two men in it, burning its way down the sky with the rear gunner slapping at the flames.

"The man is a monster," the newspaperman said. "The Germans would be justified in considering us barbarians if they could hear him talk."

Mannock, however, was not a monster. He wrote tender letters to his mother on his grimmest days at the front, sent her money regularly and sent money to his brother to buy her presents. He was dedicated to the men of his flight and risked his life many times to pull them out of trouble. He played his violin in the mess and was father-confessor to young pilots who were worried about one problem or another. His obsession with fire undoubtedly had fear in it because he admitted calmly that he carried a loaded revolver with him on every flight so that "if I am ever set on fire in the air, I can blow my brains out."

"I never believed that Mick liked to burn anybody or kill anybody, although I heard him talk," a fellow pilot said. "If he hadn't talked himself into a big hate he couldn't have done the job he had to do."

That may have been it, but Mannock is difficult to explain. He was a lover of gruesome souvenirs and that, too, turned people against him. He would jump on a motorcycle, full of excitement when he shot down a plane on his own side of the lines, and race over shell-battered roads for incredible distances to reach it. He not only cut patches of linen and crosses from downed planes as other pilots did; he stripped souvenirs from the bodies of the dead Germans, goggles, insignia, buttons from their uniforms. On one occasion he had to travel over a stretch of recently-captured territory to reach one of his victims and he saw the body of a dead German infantryman with a bayonet protruding from his chest. Mannock drew the bayonet out and sent to his brother "to keep for me till after the war."

On April 30, 1918 he was flying with Dolan, one of his flight, and Dolan shot down a German two-seater inside the British lines. The German pilot managed to land his crippled plane under control and the two Germans climbed out of their ships while the victorious Dolan and Micky Mannock circled above them. To Dolan's horror, Mannock dived on the helpless Germans and machine gunned them to death. Dolan, white-faced, walked up to Mannock the moment they landed.

"That was monstrous, Mick," he said. "Those men were prisoners of war when they landed behind our lines and stepped out of their ship.

Mannock swore impatiently. "I take no prisoners," he said.

Those were the tales that followed Mannock and dimmed his fame. Those who wrote about other pilots freely and acclaimed them, tightened their lips when they ran down the stories about Mannock. Whatever he did, he was not their type of hero.

Hero or not, Mannock paid a terrible toll in nerves and physical well-being for his achievements. His last leave in England was not a happy one. He was sick and depressed and he did not relax except with McCudden who was also on leave and whom he saw often. There was a genuine friendship between the two men, but Mannock's letters reveal the fact that he now considered McCudden a rival. One of his avowed ambitions was to beat McCudden's score, to top him in victories. It was the old urge to prove that he was "as good as any man."

McCudden could still relax lightheartedly away from the front and he had one date with a girl which may have changed his destiny and Mannock's. She was a pretty little blonde who had been regularly dating one of the American pilots who had trained in England and who was assigned to a British squadron.

The little blonde forgot her American when she had a chance to go dancing at the Savoy with the great and glittering British ace, but the American did not forget McCudden. He damned him wherever he went and spread dislike of the gay "Mac" among all of his friends. Many months later, Major W. A. Bishop, V.C., Commander of 85 Squadron, in which the Americans served, was recalled to England after his seventy-second victory. He made a farewell address and mentioned that his successor would probably be Mannock or McCudden.

The Americans had probably forgotten why they disliked McCudden but several voices were raised at once. "Get us Mannock," they said.

The 85th Squadron got Mannock and they were never disappointed in him. From his first day he justified all that they had heard of him as a leader. He talked to them as a group, outlining his philosophy of warfare and promising them that he would take care of them if they obeyed orders. He took them out singly and in groups and he shot down German planes in coldly-scientific demonstrations of how it was done, and he set up situations for other men to score victories. He led them to battle and he brought them safely home.

He was a far cry now from the old carelessly-attired Mannock who used to fraternize with the mechanics as fellow workingmen. He took a spit-and-polish pride in his uniform and he commanded the squadron and everyone in it; he was now a Major in the

R.A.F. with a row of ribbons representing his decorations. His personal score mounted as he whipped this new squadron into the shape of his desiring, but he no longer had a rival in McCudden.

Jimmy McCudden, posted to the command of 60 Squadron, crashed into a tree while flying to his new command and was killed, victim of an accident after four years of aerial warfare.

Mannock was no longer self-conscious about his bad eye, although he still avoided cameras. The strain of so much flying had fixed that useless left eye in a stare and many people believed that he had a glass eye. He had the affection and esteem of a squadron as he had had of a flight, and it pleased him. He played his violin and he argued less, but his hatred of Germans did not abate and he still had strange obsessions.

His score stood at 72 as he went on stage for the last act, equal with Bishop who had destroyed more enemies in the air than any other Englishman before the coming of Mannock. The tall Irishman had achieved his goals. He had done a good job, had far surpassed the score of Jimmy McCudden, had tied Bishop and proved himself "as good as any man."

There is something chilling in the way his biographer, "Taffy" Jones, who served with him and who minimized all his faults while magnifying his virtues, describes the next-to-last scene.

"Mannock was explaining, *amid roars of laughter,* what it felt like to be shot down in flames. He suddenly said to the little New Zealander who was a comparatively new arrival, "Have you got a Hun yet, Inglis?"

When he discovered that Inglis had not yet scored a victory, he promised to get him one. The two men took off in the dawn the next morning. It was a favorite hunting time for Mannock, seeking the hapless two-seaters whose job it was to fly low over the British lines to report on the result of the night's bombardment. The date was July 26, 1918 and at 5:30 a.m. Mannock led his protégé down on an observation plane near Merville on the German side of the lines.

According to the plan that he had outlined to Inglis in advance, Mannock dived beneath the enemy ship and zoomed, firing into it and forcing it to turn. That was Inglis' cue and he came down on top, firing. The two-seater burst into flames and Inglis pulled up, flying over it. He saw Mannock below him, turning for home.

Inglis came around in a fast bank to follow him when, suddenly, like the German ship of only seconds before, the S.E. of Micky Mannock was a mass of flames. If Mannock had his revolver with him in the cockpit he never had a chance to use it. His ship blazed through two turns of a spin and went into the ground.

Micky Mannock was dead, and in dying he was still a mystery. No man knew what killed him. Was he the victim of some lucky rifleman on the ground, of the gunner in the German ship who got in one fatal burst before he died, or of some bit of flaming wreck-

Col. William A. Bishop, V.C., who scored 72 victories and lived to wear a bowler hat in London after the war. Maj. Edward Mannock, V.C., was killed while setting up a German two-seater for a young pilot, Lt. Donald C. Inglis. Inglis shot the two-seater down but gave the credit to Mannock in his combat report, making Mannock the top British ace with 73 victories.

W. E. Barrett Collection

age that set his own ship on fire? No one knew for sure and no one was ever to know.

The spot where Mannock fell was embattled territory, fought over in the day and bombarded by night. The Germans found him and buried him, as they reported through the central prisoners of war committee, but in that shell-shattered area his grave was never located.

A German officer removed his watch and personal possessions from his body, obtained his brother's address from his wallet and sent this last group of Mannock souvenirs through the Red Cross to his home in England. *None of these personal possessions showed any trace of exposure to fire.*

Mannock's body was obviously not consumed by flames. Did he jump, unseen by Inglis, when the first dreaded tongue of flame leaped at him? No one will ever know.

How did Mannock die? In the end, we know only this: that his death received little notice in the press of the world which reported in great detail the passing of lesser men. His fame rested mainly on cold statistics without details. In his home city of Canterbury, his only memorial is the mere listing of his name on the war monument with the names of all the others from Canterbury who served in the war; an absolute equality which should delight his socialistic soul.

In 1934, sixteen years after the end of the war, a British magazine was unable to locate a picture of Mannock or sufficient information about him to answer inquiries. The editors were forced to appeal to readers of the publication for information and, if possible, a picture of "that little-known hero, Major 'Micky' Mannock, V.C."

Nevertheless, in later histories of the war, Major Edward Mannock is listed in British fashion with the initials, V.C., D.S.O., M.C. after his name. In England, these medals—Victoria Cross, Distinguished Service Order and Military Cross—are equivalent to our Congressional Medal of Honor, Distinguished Service Cross and Silver Star.

Micky Mannock, they say, gave away many victories that he might have claimed as his own; gave them, generously, to young pilots who needed encouragement. If so, with the gift of a single victory a young pilot paid all debts. Lieutenant Donald C. Inglis, who had never won a combat in the air, wrote the combat report on Mannock's last flight and he credited the destruction of the German two-seater to his commander.

That was Mannock's seventy-third victory, one more than Bishop scored. It put him at the top of the list: Great Britain's Ace of Aces. •

National Archives

German Archy: Many historians have attributed Mannock's death to German antiaircraft, but there is no way of knowing exactly what caused his plane to burn. It was difficult for Archy gunners to make claims or to prove them, but many mysterious war deaths in the air may have been due to antiaircraft—including Ball, Guynemer, Dorme.

René Fonck
The Stork Who Sought Glory

By William E. Barrett

THERE are many ways to get World War I fans arguing, but to date none is more sure-fire than the mention of one name: René Fonck. Accepted and honored by his contemporaries and historians as a crack pilot with plenty of courage and skill, Fonck's name is still beclouded because he couldn't stand mere success. The official records credit him with 75 kills. He always claimed 127 and because he did, many have doubted the validity of the 75. Never once did he withdraw a victory claim no matter how ridiculous—and some were ridiculous beyond belief.

These are the actions of a man who, not able to earn glory, had to steal it. But Fonck was not such a man. He won the *Croix de Guerre,* the *Médaille Militaire,* the Cross of the *Légion d' Honneur,* 28 other citations from the French government and a basketful of awards from other countries. All in all, they added up to enough honor for a squadron, but not for Fonck. He had to be the greatest—even if it meant claiming near-miracles. These he claimed.

On many occasions he said his plane had never been hit by a German bullet. On one occasion he recanted and said, yes, he had once been hit in a wing by *one* bullet. One bullet, and no more.

There was nothing to mark René Fonck different in the beginning. When the war broke out, he was one of millions of French boys called

RENE FONCK

to arms, the son of an ordinary family in an ordinary small town.

He was 20 when he was called up as a conscript on August 22, 1914 and assigned, at his own request, to the aviation branch of the army. He was nine months older than Georges Guynemer with whom he has been most often compared, and he was accepted for flight training five months earlier than Guynemer. Sent to the second aviation group at Dijon, he passed his qualifying examination as a pilot in April 1915.

In contrast to the tall, sickly Guynemer, Fonck was short, stocky, powerful—an athlete who exercised every day according to his own system, even in the service where most men complained of too much exercise. Guynemer was quick, volatile, restless, nervous; Fonck was slow, cautious, reserved, seemingly without nerves. Guynemer was reckless and made many mistakes as a student pilot; Fonck rarely made a mistake and earned his wings with a school record that was almost perfect. Yet, Guynemer, starting later, reached the front first in Escadrille M.S.3, June 8, 1915; Fonck went to the front in Escadrille C.47 on June 15.

As the pilot of a Caudron two-seater used for reconnaissance, Fonck quickly distinguished himself as a cool pilot who did not panic under fire. He was cited in the dispatches after two months of front-line flying for continuing a flight low over the German trenches under heavy fire and landing his observer safely with the plane badly damaged. He was cited again in November for conspicuous courage and skill.

At the time air fighting was developing as a military science in late 1915, Fonck's desire for personal attention seemed to increase. In the lull following the Champagne offensive, he took off in his Caudron without an observer and flew in the direction of the lines. He lacked a reasonable objective since he had no one with him to photograph or make notes and no weapons save the carbine that he often carried in the cockpit.

When he returned, he told a thrilling tale of a disconnected gas line, a fast landing behind the German lines before his gas ran out, a swift emergency repair and a take-off under fire with a German cavalry patrol galloping down on him. None of his amused comrades believed him—and he did not receive a mention in the dispatches for this exploit—but he insisted it was true.

That was the first indication of the shadow Fonck, the man who could not be content with what he had honestly achieved, the man with an insatiable appetite for applause.

On March 1, 1916 he turned in a vaguely-worded victory claim over a German two-seater which allegedly fell behind the enemy lines. He was accompanied by an observer, Adjutant Jaunaut, who presumably did the shooting although Fonck did not say so. The claim was disallowed for lack of confirming evidence but Fonck entered the "victory" in his log and it appears as number one in *his* list of 127.

Through the long, hard summer of 1916 Fonck continued to give a good account of himself, flying the dangerous photography and observation patrols which brought death

René Fonck (left), French ace of aces, and Maj. Georges Thenault, commanding officer of the Lafayette Escadrille. Fonck entered the air service and flew every year of the war. He was officially credited with a total of 75 victories, but he claimed a much higher figure—127.

Underwood & Underwood

to so many men and glory to so few. In midsummer his single-engine Caudron was replaced by the twin-engine Caudron and Fonck mounted a machine gun in his ship during July, fixed to fire forward through the clear area between the two propeller arcs. On the sixth of August, with Lieutenant Thiberge as his observer, Fonck gave battle to a German Rumpler and shot it down with his front gun. There was no doubt about this victory because the Rumpler landed behind the French lines and its crew became prisoners of war.

René Fonck received the *Croix de Guerre* with palm and the *Médaille Militaire* as a reward for this feat and for his consistently good record as a pilot.

After that experience Fonck was never again happy as a reconnaissance pilot. His ache to be a fighter pilot was so great he sought combat in his clumsy Caudron. On October 14 he made a highly questionable victory claim which was disallowed. This added to the reputation he was making as a fabricator of incredible adventures and hair-raising escapes. What made his posturing even harder to believe was his personality, or lack of it. He was quiet, a poor mixer, contributing little to the conversation in the mess apart from his accounts of his own exploits. He spent long hours alone, did not drink and had the habit of taking naps after every patrol. He started and finished each day with setting-up exercises, a solemn performance which the carelessly-conditioned Caudron crews found highly amusing.

The spring of 1917 was a period of intense aerial activity and new German pursuit ships —faster and more heavily armed than anything on the front—appeared on the scene. On March 17, Fonck, in the same old Caudron, was surprised along with another Caudron by five Albatroses. Fonck handled the big twin-engined ship like a scout, repeatedly shaking off and evading his attackers. The other Caudron was in trouble and Fonck dived through the three Albatroses which were ringing it. He held his ship at the point of stall as he came out of his dive above the combat while his observer, Lieutenant Marcaggi, coolly shot down one of the Germans.

This move saved the day, the French hides and won René Fonck an official victory. (His observer was credited also—the French system at that time permitting dual credit.) Fonck was cited again in the dispatches and awarded a two-week leave.

When he returned from his furlough, his greatest reward awaited him—the news that he had been released forever from the Caudrons.

On April 25, 1917 Fonck reported at Bonnemaison near Fismes, assigned to a Spad in the famous "Storks" which had been newly expanded to four escadrilles under the command of Captain Brocard. It was the dream of his life come true, the dream of any young Frenchman's life. *Les Cigognes* [the Storks] were a legendary group, the most renowned fighting crew in France.

At the time that Fonck joined them, the Storks included: Spad 3, the original Storks commanded by Captain Auger and including Dorme and Guynemer; Spad 26 commanded by Lieutenant de la Tour; Spad 73 under Captain Deullin, and Spad 103 to which Fonck was assigned under Captain d'Harcourt. Guynemer had 36 victories, Dorme 20, Delorme 21, Nungesser 21, Deullin 14, Pinsard 10, Tarascon 10 and Madon 9. In such company René Fonck was a mere cadet, but he had behind him 600 hours of Caudron time over the lines, four citations and a British decoration. He was confident, unawed, cool almost to the point of coldness.

René's first patrol with Spad 103, April 28, 1917, was a three-man sortie over the lines. A short brush with a flight of German Fokkers resulted in no fatalities for either side. On May 3, Fonck reverted to his old habits.

He flew a two-man patrol with Lieutenant Gigodot who had been assigned to familiarize him with the area. Fonck lost Gigodot and reported back alone with a long, detailed account of a combat with a German two-seater which he described as going down under his guns. Telephone calls to French balloon stations and observation posts along the front elicited no confirmation and the claim was disallowed.

Two days later, May 5, Fonck flew with three other members of S. 103: Haegelen, Hervet and Schmitter. They were attacked by four Albatros scouts which had the advantage of surprise and a wild dogfight ensued with everyone maneuvering frantically and firing at anything that looked like a target. One German plane went down in the melee and the four French ships, happy to escape from a disadvantageous position, flew home. When they landed, the other three pilots, senior to Fonck, made their reports first, stating that one Albatros had gone down but that, since everyone was firing, it was impossible to say when it was hit or by whom. Such reports were often made and in such cases, cards were cut to decide which pilot received credit. Fonck, reporting last, calmly claimed the victory and was credited with it.

Fonck shot a Rumpler down in flames on May 11. It was his fifth official victory.

On May 21, before going on the leave permitted to a man who has just become an ace, Fonck turned in another victory claim that could not be verified.

Two days after Fonck left the escadrille, "Père" Dorme disappeared while on patrol and all attempts to find a trace of his plane or his body failed. On his return, Fonck was sensitive to the general atmosphere of depression. Men talked endlessly of Dorme, recalling incidents about him, remarks that he had made. There was general agreement that his official score of 23 did not do him justice. Those who had served long with him recalled his aversion to paper work, his carelessness in entering claims and combat reports, his generosity in passing credit to young pilots for victories that he might have claimed for himself. Although he had not known Dorme long nor well, Fonck joined these discussions —and one day announced calmly that he would avenge Dorme.

The statement merely raised eyebrows. On the day that Dorme disappeared, Guynemer had shot down four German planes, all confirmed victories, and every man in the four escadrilles had been flying and fighting grimly ever since. The Storks had not waited for the return of Fonck to avenge Dorme.

Oddly enough, Fonck did, to some extent, what he vowed to do. On the morning of June 12, he dived out of the sun on two Albatros scouts which had swooped low in a hunt for French observation planes. He destroyed one of them with a single burst and tumbled it into a kitchen area behind the French trenches. The pilot was a Jasta leader, Captain von Baer, an ace with 12 victories.

For a while after that, Fonck went slightly into eclipse. French aerial losses were heavy and Germans were hunting in packs. Solo patrols were discouraged and Captain d'Harcourt of Spad 103 ordered more patrols at full strength. This hurt Fonck who never excelled when he flew with others. After that victory of June 12, he did not score again during June or July, although he put in claims for three victories that could not be verified with a fourth on August 2.

National Archives

THE STORK WHO SOUGHT GLORY

In the meantime, Guynemer was running up his score despite one invalid leave from the front. Nungesser, too, was adding to his score despite time out with wounds. Guynemer had 50 victories at the end of July and Nungesser had 30. During this time Deullin, Matton and Auger were shot down—Matton and Auger killed. Fonck merely flew, a good pilot but not one of the great ones.

The second battle of Flanders which opened July 31 made heavy demands upon the air service and, with good weather, the air activity was intense. During August René Fonck was credited officially with five of the nine victories he claimed.

Captain Heurtaux, out of action with wounds that he received on May 5, had returned to Spad 3 as commander in July, and celebrated his return by leading a raid on the German infantry moving up to relieve the troops in the trenches. This became a regular task of the Storks from that point on. But the job was confined to volunteers, as was the attacking of balloons. Fonck never volunteered for any of these assignments.

Heurtaux was shot down again on September 3 and Guynemer became commanding officer of Spad 3. Guynemer, worn out from constant flying and disliking the responsibilities of command, was morose and irritable.

The Caudron G-3 A-2 (below) was a predecessor to the twin-engine G-4 which Fonck flew in Escadrille C.47 in 1915. He allegedly scored his first victory in the G-4, a score appearing on *his* list only. Adjutant Jaunaut presumably did the shooting, although Fonck neglected to say he did.

RENÉ FONCK

The weather was bad, prohibitive for flying, and the Storks were daily expecting their transfer to another front. The general atmosphere of the four escadrilles was gloomy.

On September 11, the incomparable Guynemer flew out over the front and vanished.

The first tangible clue to his fate appeared in the form of a letter published in a German newspaper. A German pilot named Wissemann, writing to his mother, claimed that he had shot down the great Guynemer. He gave the date of his victory as September 10, however, and the French indignantly rejected his claim as the vain boast of an opportunist. Guynemer had disappeared on the eleventh.

The Storks began a crusade to avenge Guynemer, and René Fonck, in the two weeks following Guynemer's loss, claimed six victories of which three were confirmed. With his usual lack of tact he outraged the veteran Storks in doing so.

Guynemer had a distinctive sky signature, a method peculiarly his own, of announcing victories. When he returned from a patrol on which he had downed an enemy plane, he circled his own drome, rapidly opening and closing the throttle, producing a cadence, a song that sounded like: *"J'en ai un."* (I have one of them.) After his victory of September 14, René Fonck announced it as Guynemer had always announced his.

The veterans resented it. There could never be another Guynemer and some of them reproached Fonck that night in a manner typically French—by indirection, recounting stories of Guynemer's attacks on German troops and on balloons, his reckless gambling of his own life against odds and his scrupulous combat reports which underplayed his own deeds.

Fonck listened without replying. Nobody could embarrass him by telling how other men performed deeds that he would not attempt. He wrote later, in his book *Mes Combats* that "I have not assisted frequently in the burning of a balloon but it is a moving spectacle which one never forgets when one has witnessed it. I do not like thus to combat the enemy and I prefer to leave such attacks to specialists."

As had happened after the disappearance of Dorme, fate stepped in on the side of Fonck, helping him to silence his critics. On September 30, the last day on the Flanders front for the Storks, Fonck surprised a German two-seater and shot it down behind the French lines. The pilot was identified by his papers as *Leutnant* Wissemann, the man who had claimed Guynemer.

That was Fonck's fifteenth official victory and the turning point of his life.

There was no question in Fonck's mind that he, personally, was the avenger of Guynemer and the great Stork's logical successor. He forgot that Wissemann had given the wrong date in claiming that he had conquered Guynemer. In time others forgot it. Fonck was interviewed by many newspaper and magazine writers and there was no reticence in him when talking of his own exploits. He ignored the official count of

Roland Garros (left) with René Fonck. Garros, the most noted pilot in the French Air Service in 1915, spent years in German prison camps before escaping in 1918, the year in which Fonck became the great ace of France. Garros returned to active duty and was killed in action Oct. 5, 1918. René Fonck survived the war.

Underwood & Underwood

victories and told interviewers that he had 30 victories. Many papers printed his claim without explaining, perhaps without knowing that it was merely a claim. Since Guynemer had been credited with 53 victories officially at the time of his death, Fonck's claim of 30 lifted him to the position of challenger where the actual count of 15 would have been unimpressive. He was given a leave in Paris to celebrate and the timing was perfect for him.

It is an interesting point that up to this date the real Fonck and the shadow Fonck seemed to be competing and evenly balanced. He had 15 official victories and he claimed exactly 15 which were unconfirmed. From that date on, once he convinced himself that he was Guynemer's successor, Fonck became less a split personality and more frankly a glory hunter. He did not stop making wild claims, but he made a greater effort to have them acknowledged.

The newly created air ministry had taken over in the face of severe criticism of the air service, its record, its administration and the ships in which Frenchmen flew. Nungesser, the logical successor to Guynemer, was recovering from the latest of many wounds and a new hero was needed to take the minds of people off French aerial defeats.

Fonck became that hero.

Though René did not have the romantic appearance of the tall, pale Guynemer, he had solid assets. He had no bad habits and it was unlikely that he would ever embarrass the service as did the colorful and dashing Navarre who raised disturbances in Paris bars. With a talent for attracting attention to himself, René Fonck was a man worth exploiting.

Fonck knew that he had made a good impression at headquarters and he came back to his escadrille with the confidence that he could write his own rules.

One of Fonck's first acts was to request Guynemer's Cannon Spad. Guynemer had talked the Spad factory into building him a ship with a 37 mm cannon that fired through the propeller hub. It never came up to his expectations and other pilots who tried it were critical of it, but it was widely publicized and it became a Guynemer symbol.

Although it gave Fonck trouble, too, and required frequent repairs, it served to associate his name with that of Guynemer. (After the war, he stated that seven of his official victories were scored in this ship.)

The new drome of the Storks was at Chaudin near Soissons. Fonck celebrated his return to the escadrille from Paris with a solo patrol on October 10 and the claim that he had destroyed two German scouts. There was no confirmation. On October 12 he claimed another which was not confirmed. On October 15 he claimed three, two of which were confirmed. In the next two weeks he claimed three more, receiving credit for two.

Winter was settling down hard over the trenches and there was little air activity. René Fonck had 20 official victories so he applied for a long leave of absence, married a girl from his home town and went on a honeymoon. He did not come back to the front until January 1918.

At this time the Storks were flying over the old Verdun battlefield. Captain Hormant had replaced Brocard as commander. On his first patrol over this front, Fonck flew with Captain d'Harcourt, Lieutenant Fontaine, and two young pilots. Captain d'Harcourt was forced to drop out of formation with engine trouble and, shortly afterwards, Fontaine led the two youngsters down on a couple of German two-seaters while Fonck flew above them. Fontaine got into trouble immediately when a burst from a German observer's gun silenced his engine. Fonck swooped down, set the German aflame with one burst and, concerned for the inexperienced pilots who had separated in their futile attack on the other German, gave them the signal to follow him and led them home.

Fonck referred to this incident several times later when he was questioned about his avoidance of regular patrols. As he wrote in his book: "I preferred to fly alone; thus I was able to have more adventures comfortably because I was not afraid of putting comrades less experienced than myself in a bad position. It was when alone that I performed those little coups of audacity which amused me."

In February, he amused himself with many of these "little coups of audacity," claiming eight victories and receiving credit for five. In March he claimed 11, seven of which were confirmed.

RENÉ FONCK

The matter of confirmations was much simplified under the system inaugurated by the new air ministry which was eager to confront its political critics with evidence of French superiority in the air. The Storks now had a *homologuer* whose duty it was to follow up every victory claim entered by phoning front positions or by a personal visit to the front if necessary.

René Fonck worked this individual harder than all of the other Storks combined. His combat reports were always sketchy and he was insistent upon confirmation for every claim.

With each success, Fonck became more of a prima donna. He declared that two hours of front-line flying was sufficient if a pilot did his work well, and he confined himself to two hours most days even when his comrades were flying much more than that. He was a Stork but a special case, fighting his own war in his own way, pointing to his mounting score as the answer to all criticism.

"Flying and fighting in the air," he said, "calls for fine physical condition and one must stay in training as for an athletic event. It is folly to fly to the point of fatigue or to risk one's life when one is not feeling physically fit."

This was, no doubt, sound philosophy, but it was not the statement of a man who was all out to win the war; it was the frank statement of a glory hunter concerned only with his own personal record.

He claimed six victories in April and the best efforts of the *homologuer* confirmed only three of them. When the French press belatedly reported that Captain J. L. Trollope of the Royal Flying Corps had shot down six German planes in one day during March, Fonck could talk of little else. "One would have to have it in his mind that he wanted to shoot six," Fonck said. "There would have to be the intent."

The other pilots laughed, shrugged and yawned. Such talk was nonsense.

On May 9, 1918 Fonck found himself flying in company with Captain Battle and Lieutenant Fontaine. As they crossed the lines they spotted a German two-seater protected by two Fokkers. Fonck led the attack, diving down on the nearest Fokker and shooting him out of the sky with a single burst. Continuing his dive, Fonck pulled out under the two-seater and zoomed, literally hanging by his prop as he poured two bursts into it.

The second Fokker pilot, with the advantage of altitude now, dived on Fonck who fell off on one wing, avoiding his fire. Fonck then dived below the German and, zooming up under him as he came out of his dive, destroyed him with one long burst.

"It was all over in five seconds," Fonck said.

Three German planes containing four men were tumbling down the sky before the astonished Fontaine and Battle who had been

U. S. Signal Corps

René Fonck with Georges Carpentier. This photograph was taken during a boxing tournament behind the lines. Carpentier, light heavyweight champion of France, enlisted in the French Air Service at the outbreak of the war, serving as aviation signal officer and observer. He was decorated twice and mentioned three times in dispatches. After the war Carpentier fought Jack Dempsey for the world heavyweight championship and was knocked out in four rounds.

only a trifle slow in following Fonck in his dive.

There was no question about confirmation on those three planes and Fonck, hot for further battle, landed on his own drome only long enough to put gas in his tank and check his guns. He had three victories for the day and there was daylight left. He had "the intent" to shoot down six.

To Fonck's great annoyance, Brugère and Thouzelier joined him when he took off, flying behind him. He gained altitude as he flew toward the lines and a cloud floor moved in under him. Through a rift in the clouds he spotted a German two-seater below him and dived. He raked the enemy ship from the observer's roost to the prop before either of the Germans knew that they were not alone in the soupy sky.

He cruised just under the clouds after the two-seater went down and a flight of Fokkers materialized below him followed almost immediately by five Albatroses flying slightly higher.

"I hesitated to attack," Fonck wrote, "but the desire to complete my performance overcame my prudence and I chose to risk combat."

Aiming his Spad at the gap between the two flights, he dived full out. Waiting until the rearmost Fokker was huge in his sights, he laid a burst into the cockpit. The Fokker fell under his diving ship, turning wing over wing before plunging straight toward earth. At that instant the five Albatroses dived.

Fonck came out of his own dive and zoomed into the oncoming Germans. He shot the leader down in flames without leveling out of his zoom and was in the clouds again before his foes had time to fire a single burst.

This second trio of Fonck's day landed within the French lines and his "sextuple" was confirmed before he landed on his own drome. In getting his six, he demonstrated conclusively that, when he wanted to be, there was no more dangerous man on the front.

Still Fonck had to claim too much. In writing of his big day, he stated:

"My sextuple victory of May 1918 had stupefied my contemporaries. The enemy, terror-stricken, did not for several days recover his self-possession, and, on our side, enthusiasm overflowed."

If the Germans were stupefied or terror-stricken the statistics do not reveal it. In that month of May 1918 the German Imperial Air Force destroyed 413 Allied planes and 23 balloons at a loss of 180 of their own planes.

Fonck, however, preferred to believe that he had won his war for the month. He basked in glory and flew seldom. When he did go out he brought back tales of combat and conquest, claiming single victories on May 12 and 18, a double on the fifteenth. The poor *homologuer* phoned all over, but the claims were not confirmable.

On the nineteenth, Fonck had two confirmations out of three claims. He took off for Paris the next day and was, as usual, interviewed by the press. He repeated a claim he had first made in an interview on April 3, 1918, updated now with added victories.

"I have destroyed 80 enemy airplanes in combat," he said, "and I have never received a bullet in my machine. No German pilot has succeeded in hitting me once."

He had, at that time, 44 confirmed victories and 36 unverified claims but, in typical Fonck fashion, he added them together, never relinquishing a claim that he had made. Eighty was the magic figure reached by Baron Manfred von Richthofen before his death in April and it was far in excess of the scores achieved by the immortal Guynemer, or the Britishers Ball and McCudden; all of whom had been bested many times in combat, shot down, or forced to fly home in badly-riddled ships. This new wonder claimed to have surpassed them all.

Fonck's own comrades were not enthusiastic. The ghost of the beloved Guynemer still lingered. Fonck, who deserved acclaim, received it, but pilots did not quite believe in him and the people of France did not take him to their breasts as they had Guynemer. Fonck seemed oblivious of this. He extended his leave into the middle of June, celebrated his return with a very doubtful and unconfirmed victory claim, then scored an authentic and confirmed triple victory in one day. He claimed five more victories that month and two of them were confirmed.

Fonck's combat reports, always vague, became even more confusing. He had never had a sharp eye for enemy models and hardly ever attempted to identify the make or model of a two-seater. He identified enemy scouts as "fighter planes," occasionally naming them Albatros or Fokker (which he spelled "Focker"). He claimed, perhaps rightly, that he could not tell where a plane would land when shot down at 20,000 feet.

Some of the skeptics insisted, however, that the Fonck method was a shotgun system of gambling for credit. A vaguely-described airplane destroyed where no one saw the combat, which might land anywhere, was at least a good bet for confirmation during a period of heavy air fighting if a harassed, hard-pressed *homologuer* was working for the confirmation.

"He robs the dead," one pilot said, and his meaning was plain. German planes that crashed by accident or were shot down by Frenchmen who were killed or wounded before they turned in combat reports were credited to Fonck because he made his reports a basket big enough to receive them.

Fonck had seven confirmed victories and four unverified claims in July, four victories and three doubtful claims in August. After the last of these questionable and unverified claims on August 15, he took another long vacation.

During Fonck's absence the doubts that he had inspired grew and spread. Young and obscure pilots scored victories which they claimed would never have been credited to them if Fonck were still flying. He had an uncanny knack, they claimed, of spotting a dogfight or an attack on a two-seater from the heights at which he flew, and a habit of diving down after a kill had been made, or while a confused battle was in progress, firing his guns and claiming every ship that fell. One of his triple victories, it was rumored, occurred in just this manner, with Fonck claiming every ship knocked down in a dogfight which he joined late; his prestige reinforcing his claim.

Fonck, in his book, describes several such fights, claiming that his entry into the battle was a rescue operation. He might have been

U. S. Signal Corps

correct in his claim. He did kill swiftly with little waste fire, and less experienced pilots could easily underestimate him.

In late September René Fonck returned to the Storks bronzed and fit and rested. He was incapable of imagining that people would doubt him, so he probably suspected nothing of the fact that his reputation had been bounced around in his absence. On September 26, 1918 however, he wrote an answer in the air; an answer not entirely in his favor.

The German army was breaking up and in full retreat. René Fonck flew alone from the Stork drome at Noblette, north of Chalons. Although he had never in his entire career gone down on a balloon, his guns, by his own admission, were loaded with incendiary ammunition. Climbing into the morning sun, he discovered five Fokkers beneath him and dived. They were flying in a V and it was his usual tactic to pick off one of the rearmost ships in a surprise attack. On this occasion the pilot of the Fokker behind the leader and on his right was the only one to sense danger. He turned his head, then poured gas to his engine, moving up to attract his leader's attention. Fonck shot him across the other ship which he had first selected for his victim, then, swerving slightly, shot the rearmost plane. Both of the Fokkers flamed and Fonck zoomed away before the three shocked survivors could come around and give him battle.

As he climbed again, Fonck saw a French antiaircraft battery in action and flew to investigate. A German two-seater was flying in and out of the Archy bursts and Fonck approached to within 30 meters of it without being observed. He killed the observer with a single shot and the alarmed pilot dived so suddenly that the body of the observer was thrown free.

Fonck, pulling out of his dive to attack again, looked up and was horrified to see the corpse of the observer that he had killed hurtling down upon him. He banked sharply and the plummeting body missed his wing by inches. Shaking off his shock, Fonck pursued the fleeing two-seater and sent it down in flames.

He had three victories, easy confirmations since all of them burned, and the day was young.

Fonck flew out again in the late afternoon. He flew alone and the sky was filled with desperate Germans. He saw a far-away flight of Fokkers go down upon a group of Spads and disperse them. Below him was a patrol of three Spads from his own escadrille piloted by Fontaine, Loup and Brugère. Fonck joined them as the victorious Fokkers, fresh from combat, closed in. There were five Fokkers and four Spads. Three more Fokkers came down and then another Spad, all joining in the tail-chasing contest that developed. The lone Spad was identifiable by his insigne as Captain de Sevin of Spad 26, who was the survivor of the earlier fight.

Captain de Sevin and Brugère were in trouble and Fonck shot down two Fokkers to extricate them, just as De Sevin went down.

Five Albatroses appeared below the fight and Fonck dived alone to intercept them before they could join the attack. As he opened fire on the Albatros, a Fokker, shot down by one of the other pilots, tumbled down in

The Spad 7, a sturdy ship built for maneuvering and outdueling the enemy, was the favorite of *Les Cigognes* (the Storks) to which Fonck reported in April 1917 as a member of Spad 103. The ship at left is the Spad 13, successor to the 7, and the ship in which many American aces flew to glory in the war.

RENE FONCK

flames, barely missing Fonck who, in banking sharply, brushed the wing of an Albatros with his wheels. He destroyed that crippled Albatros with one burst and pulled out of the fight with jammed guns.

"If my guns had not failed me," he wrote, "I am confident that I could have wiped out the Albatroses and surpassed my previous record."

As it was, he returned to his drome safely with a claim for three victories in that fight, six for the day; the second time that he had performed the feat.

Only the angels could straighten out the combat reports of that frantic, confused dogfight. Fonck was specific, however, about one fact; that he had shot down the two Fokkers with which De Sevin and Brugère were engaged, then, later, an Albatros. Fontaine shot down the flamer which narrowly missed Fonck.

There was great jubilation in Spad 103 and no problem at all about confirmations. The great Fonck had repeated his inimitable feat —six in one day.

Then, Captain de Sevin came back from the dead. Presumed killed in the fight, he regained control of his damaged plane and made a safe landing behind the advancing French troops. In his carefully written combat report, he claimed that he shot down the Fokker with which he was engaged before he himself was forced out of the fight. De Sevin was a veteran, an escadrille leader, and no maker of wild claims. This was an embarrassment, doubly embarrassing when he was informed of Fonck's claim and refused to withdraw his own.

Fonck either had his second sextuple victory, or he had a five this time, which was not as sensational. Word was on the wires already, all over France, that he had scored six times.

Capping the excitement and the confusion was the discovery of papers on the body of one of the Fokker pilots which identified him as *Leutnant* Fritz Rumey, who had compiled a fantastic record in a few short months at the front, a *Pour le Mérite* ace with 45 victories.

The French Command in its wisdom decided that René Fonck had downed six German planes on September 26 and that one of his victims was the German ace, Rumey, thus answering for Germany the question—"Who is René Fonck?"

The war did not last long after that and René Fonck was officially credited with 75 victories at the end, credited in his own book with 127. He had far surpassed the statistical record of Guynemer but he did not stand on the same pinnacle of greatness. Fonck was honored but not idolized. Several men wrote books about Guynemer; no one wrote a book about Fonck but Fonck. Several pilots of long service with the French wrote books about their experiences without once mentioning René Fonck; no one wrote about the French Air Service without mentioning Guynemer. Among the survivors, the fighting pilot's pilot was Nungesser. •

A postwar photograph of René Fonck made when he was seeking backers for an ill-fated transatlantic attempt. The plane crashed taking off.

Richard Hardin

Ernst Udet
Duel Master of the Sky

By Richard Hanser

SERGEANT-PILOT Ernst Udet of the Imperial German Air Service counted the dots on the horizon, and hurriedly wiped his goggles with one gloved hand. What he was seeing, he thought, must be oil specks thrown by the engine. But the dots kept growing in size and number until they reached an impossible 23—Caudrons and Farmans, with a huge Voisin hovering over the flock like a monstrous mother hen.

He twisted in the cockpit to scan the vast, bright sky behind. There was not a friendly plane in sight. He was alone, one against 23, confronting the first massed aerial attack in the history of war.

The oncoming French were sprawled all over the sky in no set formation. They were close enough to spot him as he started climbing to get well above them, but not a plane wavered from its course. They could afford to ignore him. Twenty-three to one.

Through the irregular pattern of the wings now below him he caught a fleeting glimpse of the earth. On the outskirts of Mühlhausen, tiny figures were running wildly about and gesticulating toward the sky in an open-air beer garden, their *gemütlich* Sunday afternoon suddenly disrupted by the enemy swarming like hornets overhead.

Directly under Udet droned a cluster of twin-engine Caudrons with a wide-winged Farman in their midst. He knew from the slamming of his heart and the moistness of his palms on the control column of his Fokker that for him the moment of supreme decision had come again. He had failed it once before. If he failed it now, he was through as a pilot and a man.

He gunned his motor, nosed over, and dived.

It seemed as if the Farman came up at him in an expanding rush, "like something under a microscope brought suddenly into focus." He could clearly see the leather crash helmet of the French observer as the enemy machine gun was tilted up at him. His first panicky impulse was to start firing at once, 80 meters away, but this time he had to be absolutely sure. He nerved himself to hold back until the distance closed to 40 meters, then 30.

Then he opened up with his twin Spandau machine guns, and the Farman seemed to lurch and shudder for an instant before a gout of flame spurted from it and it exploded. He had hit the gas tank.

A metallic tattoo was being played across his own fuselage. Two of the surrounding Caudrons had jumped him but now everything seemed to go as smoothly as in a training exercise and he reacted automatically without a flicker of fear or confusion. He dived steeply away, and when he pulled out the flaming ruins of the Farman came hurtling past. A moment lated he saw something revolving grotesquely in the sky like an enormous frog—the French observer.

"At that moment," Udet said later, "I had no feeling that that was a human being. I thought only one thing: Victory! Victory! The iron ring around my breast seemed to burst and I felt a release that was like intoxication."

By now every available fighter from his home airfield at Habsheim had scrambled into the air. The mass of French planes disintegrated into its component parts under the impact of the German counterattack, and the sky was filled with the howling of engines and clattering of machine guns as individual dogfights broke out all over the sky.

For Udet the first heady surge of triumph quickly passed, and he felt sober, cool and clearheaded. He had his first kill. He was blooded.

At the airfield he reported tersely to the

National Archives

commandant: "Sergeant-Pilot Udet, returned from combat. Two-seater Farman destroyed."

He did not look much like a conquering hero as he walked across the field to his quarters. He was of less than average height, with mild blue-gray eyes and nondescript sandy hair. He had the ruddy, rustic complexion of a ploughboy and seemed, all in all, far better fitted for the grime and drudgery of the unglamorous infantry than for the dash and derring-do of the war in the air. He had little of the outward swank and swagger which the world was beginning to associate with the astonishing new phenomenon of combat in the clouds.

The fact was, though, that this was one of the greatest of them all. For with his first kill Ernst Udet had launched himself on a career so spectacular and strange that it would make him a legend in his lifetime and an enigma afterward.

Nobody could know it at the time, and least of all himself, but at the age of 19 he was already on his way to becoming one of the most slashingly successful combat pilots of World War I, the most fabulous stunt flyer ever seen, and a maker of aviation history whose impact, in another war yet to come, would be felt with shattering effect on Warsaw, Paris and London.

But if, on that March day in 1916, he could not foresee the glitter and the glory that lay ahead, perhaps it was just as well. The ultimate agony that would one day turn everything to gall was also hidden from him.

The Habsheim command was quartered in the vacation villa of an absent American, and that night the pilots celebrated their repulse of the French attack. Ernst Udet had special reason to rejoice. He knew now that he would be able to live up to the vow he had taken months ago after his first ignominious defeat in combat. That had been an encounter with a Caudron, too, and he had frozen at the controls, sitting rigid and paralyzed in a kind of nightmare stupor as he watched the enemy approach. He and the Frenchman seemed about to pass each other at the same height without action on either side when the Caudron opened fire, and Udet felt a blow on the side of his face like the smash of a ham-

Ernst Udet (left), 62 victories, and Bruno Loerzer (right), 44 victories, with their friend Siegfried Abel. Udet was the highest-scoring German ace still surviving at the war's end. Loerzer had commanded *J.G. 3* composed of four *Jagdstaffels*.

Ernst Udet scored many of his most notable victories in Fokker triplane (left) which he flew for the first time when he joined Baron von Richthofen's Flying Circus.

mer. His goggles were shot off, and blood from the splintered glass blinded him. He turned his ship away, dived into the clouds for shelter, and ran for home.

Out of that experience had come a moral hardening far more valuable for his future than if he had won the fight. Afterward, alone in his room, he told himself in a sweat of self-reproach: "You failed because at the instant of battle you thought of yourself. You feared for your life." And then he formulated what was to be his creed of manhood from then on: "Being a soldier means thinking only of the enemy, of victory, and forgetting yourself...

"... From now on I will be nothing but a soldier."

The next day, with his mechanic, he hammered together a life-sized silhouette of a Nieuport. Every evening, after a day's duty, he had the model hauled to the center of the landing field and used it for target practice. From 300 meters up he dived his plane at the mock enemy, time after time, hour after hour, day after day, opening fire at 100 meters or less, pulling up his ship just short of the earth, climbing, turning, coming back at it again and again. He kept careful score of his hits and misses with shots in the motor counting double. Day after day he kept at it, sharpening his shooting accuracy, perfecting the precision of his flying, diving closer and ever closer to his target.

Ernst Udet was no raw novice of the air war when he suffered his first defeat and began schooling himself for his first victory. He had already been awarded the Iron Cross, Second Class, for the skillful landing of a plane with defective controls, thereby "preserving a valuable airship for the Fatherland and saving his observer's life"—not to mention his own. He had also been sentenced to seven days of military arrest for reckless flying in the crash of an Aviatik B, thereby "destroying a valuable airship for the Fatherland and gravely endangering his observer's life"—not to mention his own.

On one of these missions, flying an observation plane known as an L.V.G., he acted as pilot for a Lieutenant Hartmann who may be the unsung inventor of the bomb bay. Instead of tossing the bombs out of the cockpit, as the custom then was, Lieutenant Hartmann used a do-it-yourself arrangement which consisted of a small trap door cut into the floor of his forward cockpit. Once over the target, Hartmann opened the trap door, held the bomb perpendicularly over it, and squinted along it by way of taking aim before letting it go.

It was after this experience with two-seaters that Ernst Udet was then shifted to Habsheim and became a single-seater fighter pilot. This was the dream-come-true of every young flyer worth his salt, and when the assignment came down from staff headquarters *despite* the black mark of a prison sentence, his captain had growled: *"Mehr Glück als Verstand"*—"More luck than brains." Udet's flying luck in war and peace would become legendary around the world. And he was a man who would need all the luck he could get.

Now, instead of flying routine observation flights that merely crisscrossed the same monotonous terrain, he would be permitted to ride into battle in the sleek new fighting machines which demanded all the skill and courage that any pilot could bring to them— the devastating new Fokker D-7, or perhaps the streamlined Pfalz D-3. In contrast to the plodding observation planes, the newer ships had clean, swift lines that made them seem to be racing even while standing motionless on the ground and they answered surely and sweetly to the touch, like a fine instrument in the hands of a finished musician. Udet developed a fondness, and an affinity, for the Fokker with its two Spandau machine guns and its 160-horsepower Mercedes engine.

In such a plane a man could measure himself against the best that the enemy had to offer, and since this was a front facing the French, the best might mean the flashy René Fonck, so dapper on the ground and so deadly in the air, or even the great Georges Guynemer who always flew alone and whom the Germans called "the Richthofen of the enemy." Baron Manfred von Richthofen himself, of course, flew a Fokker—the red triplane that was the terror of the French and British alike.

But at this period not every sortie resulted in combat, and Udet often flew for weeks at a time without clashing with an enemy plane. Months passed in patrol flights and strafing missions, while the troops below remained deadlocked in the fruitless slaughter of the trenches, and the war in the air seemed to be marking time before bursting into the tempestuous climax that was coming. It was not until spring of 1917 that he became an ace with his fifth kill, a single-seater Nieuport over Chavignon, and scored his sixth a month later. By this time he was a second lieutenant and leader of a *Jagdstaffel.*

Jasta 15 took to the air from its base at Boncourt three times a day, morning, noon and evening. For some reason the opposing French were being cautious and action was rare. But when they showed themselves they were flying Spads, for which the Germans had a wholesome respect.

But day by day, the tempo of the air war mounted. Pilots who had joined the *Jagdstaffel* with Udet were being crossed off the roster. Soon he was the last survivor of the original *Jasta 15*, and then the only one left of the men who had beaten off the French mass attack at Habsheim. As he watched his comrades disappear one by one, he summed up in a vivid phrase his premonition of the fate that waited for them all:

"Death flies faster. . ."

That summer there were rumors of an Allied offensive, and the fronts were restive. All along the sector where Udet was stationed the fat observation balloons of the enemy lolled lazily, but ominously, on their tethers. He decided to get one of them.

He took off in the early morning and climbed to an unusual height for him, 5,000 meters, well into the sun in order to be able to drop unseen on his prey. The balloons were always anchored in a bristling nest of antiaircraft guns, and getting one was no picnic. Over Lierval he had singled out his target when he saw a plane approaching from the west. A lone hunter like himself. A Spad.

He settled himself in the cockpit. There would be battle.

The distance between them rapidly closed, and they began to maneuver for position in what the Allies called a dogfight and the Germans a *Kurvenkampf*—literally a "battle of curves." What looked from below like the graceful and sportive play of mating birds—the intertwined patterns of banking, dipping, rolling, soaring—was in fact the deadliest of duels. Whichever pilot allowed his adversary to get behind him was lost, and whichever achieved that position was the almost certain victor. The single-seater fighter could shoot only straight forward and was defenseless behind.

Udet soon discovered with whom it was he had to deal: Guynemer.

On the second pass he came close enough to see the thin, white face under the leather helmet, the face that was called "girlish" when

Erich Löwenhardt (below) was Udet's great rival. The competition between the two was intense with first one and then the other forging ahead in the victory column. Their rivalry was sparked by a mutual dislike. Löwenhardt was ultimately killed as Boelcke was, in a collision with a comrade. His final score was 53.

Heinz Nowarra

it was not set in the concentration of battle. He was a small and delicate man but the French called him the "giant of the air," and he had already shot down 30 Germans.

Udet was sure when, on the next pass, he saw *Le Vieux Charles*—"Old Charlie"—painted on the side of the Spad. That was Guynemer's plane, and from the way it was being handled only Guynemer could be flying it.

Udet went into a half-loop in order to get above the Spad and come down on it, but Guynemer answered with a loop of his own that negated the maneuver. The pattern was repeated when Udet tried to chandelle, an upward corkscrew climb, only to find the Spad matching it. For a split instant, as Udet came out of a bank, he was caught in Guynemer's sights and felt a splatter of bullets in one of his wings.

No matter how Udet kicked his plane around the sky, the Frenchman was close upon him, in accordance with his basic motto for combat: "I hang on to my adversary like a madman." But the converse was also true: no maneuver of the Frenchman's caught Udet unawares. His plane was never where Guynemer wanted it, and he always returned to the attack after slipping away. Like two evenly matched swordsmen, each met every thrust with its required parry, and returned to lunge and slash again.

The duel lasted eight minutes and for seconds at a time Udet was swept away by the sheer exhilaration of such glorious flying, almost forgetting in his admiration for Guynemer's skill that his own life was at stake. Then came the unexpected climax.

In another tight bank, Udet found the Frenchman momentarily in front of his guns. He pressed the trigger on his control column but there was no response from the Spandaus. Another jam.

Flying with his left hand, Udet tried with his right to adjust the ammunition belts so they would again feed smoothly into the guns. It didn't work.

Now Guynemer was at last above him, flying upside down, jockeying into position for the kill.

U. S. Air Force

In desperation, Udet took both hands off the controls and pounded furiously with both fists on the jammed machine guns. Sometimes that helped, but it didn't now.

Guynemer saw what was happening. His adversary's guns were gone. Udet was helpless.

"Then it happened," Udet reported afterwards. "I looked up to see what he would do with me now. I was at his mercy. I could hardly believe my eyes. He put out one hand, waved to me and dived away to the west, letting me fly home unhurt."

Coldly viewed, there was something foolish about that gesture by Guynemer. By waving away a sure victory he had allowed Ernst Udet to live and fight again, and Udet went on to shoot down a total of 62 Allied planes, including many piloted by Guynemer's own comrades. War as we have come to know it has no room for such romanticism. "Chivalry" has become a story-book word that belongs to a day long gone.

But at that time the action of Georges Guynemer was by no means unique. Phrases like "the knighthood of the air" had not yet become mere gabble for recruiting posters. The men who flew the planes in World War I felt themselves members of an almost mystic brotherhood that transcended fronts and boundaries. They shared in common an experience none before them had known, the challenge of exerting their skill and testing their manhood in the newly-conquered realm of space. It set them apart from all the men-at-arms of the past, and made of them a special breed.

With an almost incredible burst of flying, fighting and killing, Ernst Udet entered the magic circle of the air immortals. He had long since made himself into a skilled and dangerous pilot with a respectable score of kills; now something like genius seemed to flow into him and he became sensational.

Over Lens in Flanders, in a fabulous 20 seconds of action, he shot down three English planes out of a flight of five, and vanished untouched. He had dropped out of the sun, disposed of the rear left plane of the echelon with one five-shot burst, swept on to repeat with the next plane in line, and then climaxed his swoop by shooting the lead plane down in flames. He was gone before the remaining two could bring their guns to bear.

This was now his set style in combat: to fall like a falcon out of the sun upon an enemy flight, pick off his prey before his presence was even known, rely on surprise and confusion for his getaway. Always there was the marvelous, controlled precision of his flying, the sureness of his shooting, and the infallible instinct for action. He became known as *die Wespe*, "the Wasp," and his fame spread on both sides of the front.

In the spring of 1918 he received the ultimate accolade. He was asked to join the squadron of Baron von Richthofen.

The Baron extended the invitation personally and quite informally. He drove up unannounced in a military car and waved a greeting. "*Tag*, Udet. I've been hearing about you. What's your score now?"

"Nineteen acknowledged and another reported, Herr Baron."

"Hmm. Twenty." He gave Udet a keen, appraising look. "You ought to be about ripe for us. What do you say?"

Richthofen's command was known officially as *Jagdgeschwader N. R. 1* but more popularly as "the Flying Circus," a name derived from the bright red of the Fokkers it flew.

Udet reported to the squadron at ten o'clock one morning and by noon found himself for the first time at the controls of the highly maneuverable three-wing Fokker, flying west behind the Baron over No Man's Land as a member of *Jasta 11*.

They were about 500 meters over the ruined town of Albert when Udet spotted an English R.E. observation plane close under the clouds ahead, directing fire for the artillery. The R.E. evidently did not see the Fokkers, and continued on its business as if alone in the sky. Udet peeled off the formation.

He made his approach from in front and below. He zoomed up under the sluggish R.E.

The Fokker D-7 (left) was the standard ship of the Richthofen Circus during Hermann Goering's term of command; one of the finest single-seaters of the war. J.G. 1's fighting equipment was considerably improved with the Fokker, but Ernst Udet and others didn't care too much for Goering.

like a shark attacking its prey, sending bursts from both guns into the motor and falling away. The Englishman caught fire and spun to earth.

In less than a minute Udet had attacked, killed the plane, and resumed his place in the formation. He noted that the Baron, who missed nothing, had seen the whole performance and twisted his head to send back a curt nod of approval.

When Udet landed, the Baron was standing beside his plane waiting for him.

"Do you do that sort of thing very often, Udet—from in front and below?"

"I've had some success with it," said Udet as casually as he could.

Richthofen turned to go, but said over his shoulder: "Tomorrow you take over *Jasta 11*."

With a single flight Udet had become not only a fully accepted member of the Flying Circus but a leader of it, and before long he was its most brilliant performer after the Baron himself. He saw at once why *J. G. 1* had come to be the most spectacularly successful unit on the front.

Other outfits with which he had served were customarily stationed 20 and 30 kilometers behind the lines. Richthofen's men took off from fields which often were within range of the enemy artillery. Other pilots were comfortably quartered in castles and villages. The Richthofen flyers lived on the edge of the airfield in corrugated iron huts from where they could be summoned to com-

A victim of Udet, Lt. Walter B. Wanamaker, U.S.A.S., is lying on a stretcher behind German lines after being shot down on July 2, 1918. Udet landed nearby, offered Wanamaker a cigarette and ordered an ambulance for the wounded man. He then took this picture. Wanamaker was on the tail of Erich Löwenhardt, Udet's rival, when he became victory No. 39 for Udet.

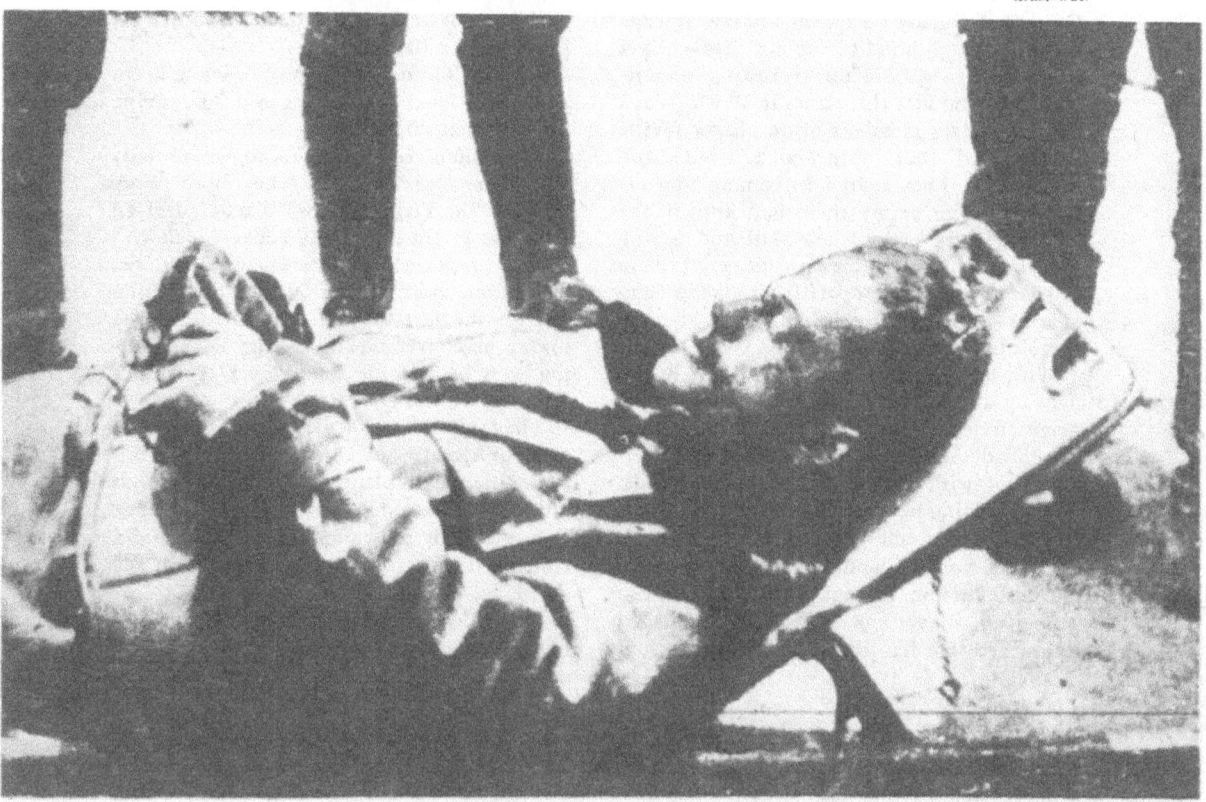

Ernst Udet

bat at a moment's notice. Other *Staffel* flew against the enemy two or three times a day, and were often grounded by bad weather. Richthofen's pilots made as many as five combat flights a day, and were seldom stopped by the elements.

They flew incessantly and as the ground fighting flared into unprecedented violence in the spring of 1918, the strain increased day by day, almost hour by hour. And it was at this time that the U. S. Air Service began to appear above the battlefields, adding fresh manpower to Allied aviation while German flying strength steadily dwindled.

Udet's first encounter with an American left a deep impression on him, though it turned out to be a comparatively easy victory.

The thudding of German flak awoke him early one morning and he ran for his plane in his night clothes, changing into flying gear as he went. Once aloft, he headed in the direction of the flak bursts which told him where the action was. The fight was already in progress—seven Fokkers against eight Nieuports.

A pilot from the squadron named Löwenhardt was hot on the tail of one of the Nieuports, oblivious of the fact that he in turn was being pursued by another Nieuport. Udet instantly added himself to the dog-eat-dog sequence by diving on Löwenhardt's attacker. It was a soft touch. He had his Nieuport in his sights before the pilot knew he was there, and the first burst sent it spinning.

But after a long drop the Nieuport managed to pull out. Then it wobbled and lurched and hit with a crash, but did not burst into flame.

Udet landed nearby and when he reached the wreckage the pilot was crawling painfully out. There was no response to Udet's greeting in French, and then he saw that this was not a Frenchman but an American who flew a French plane as many of his countrymen were doing. Udet took a longer look as he

National Archives

A photograph of Hermann Goering seated in his Fokker D.R. 1 triplane taken when he was commander of *Jasta 27*. On June 14, 1918, Goering took over command of the famous Richthofen *Jagdgeschwader* and led it until the war was over.

proffered a cigarette. What kind of men were these who had come across an ocean to fight against Germany?

The American introduced himself: Lieutenant Walter Wanamaker of Akron, Ohio. He dragged gratefully on the cigarette, and then pointed to his thigh: "Broken," he said casually.

Udet could tell that he was suffering acutely and doing his best to conceal it. He summoned medics and as they loaded the American onto a stretcher they told Udet that three other U. S. pilots had also been shot down.

Udet passed this information on to the boy from Ohio.

"Well," said Wanamaker dryly, "we're having a great morning." Then he added with a wave as they carried him off: "But don't worry. We'll do better."

Something about the American appealed to Udet. This was probably the boy's first action and he had taken a cruel beating, but he was carrying it off jauntily and with his confidence unimpaired. On a hunch, Udet got a knife and from the fabric of the ruined Nieuport he cut the plane's identification number. He kept it as a souvenir. His first American...

The strangest and most nerve-racking battle Udet ever fought occurred late one afternoon not long after when he was on patrol with another plane from the squadron. They were jumped from out of the sun by two swift, slashing S.E.5s and split apart to fight their separate fights.

Udet's man came at him head-on with both guns going. Udet in turn flew straight toward him, also firing. At the last possible moment the English plane lifted its nose and went roaring over Udet's. It came so close that Udet could feel the terrific rush of air as it passed and smell the fumes of its exhaust.

Udet banked around to face his man again. The S.E.5 had done the same.

"Now the *Kurvenkampf* begins," Udet thought. But once again, instead of maneuvering for position, they came hurtling at each other nose-and-nose, shooting as they came.

"It was," Udet reported later, "like two horsemen in a tournament riding at each other with couched lances. This time I flew over him.

"Another turn, and again he is in front of me, and again we rush directly at each other all-out. The thin white streams of the tracers hang in the sky like curtains. There is barely a hand's breadth between us when he sweeps over me as we meet. I can read the numerals painted in black on his tail: 8824.

"The same thing again for the fourth time.

German snapshot; collection of W. E. Barrett

Ernst Udet's commander, Hermann Goering (center) is flanked by Bruno Loerzer (left) and Lothar von Richthofen (right), Manfred's younger brother. While under Goering's command the Richthofen *Jagdgeschwader* scored its 500th victory, appropriately claimed by Lothar.

I feel my hands getting moist. I know I've got a man opposite me who is fighting the fight of his life. He or I . . . one or the other. Perhaps both.

"The fifth time. My nerves are tautened to the breaking point, but my head stays clear. This time the decision will have to come. I get him full in my sights, I hold my course dead at him. I am determined not to give an inch when we meet.

"A flash of memory: it was over Lens that I saw it. An air duel like this one. Two planes streaked head-on at each other, and rammed together. The fuselages folded up like accordions and fell to earth. The wings broke off and seemed to fly on for a while by themselves before fluttering to earth. . . .

"Like two wild boars we were charging at each other. If he keeps his nerve this time, we're both goners.

"Now! The moment comes and—he turns away. At the same instant my machine gun burst reaches him. His plane buckles, and something seems to throw it over on its back before it plunges to earth. I watch it hit in a shell hole and throw up a fountain of earth.

"I circle the place twice, marking the spot. Down below I see German soldiers in field-gray, jumping up and down and waving to me. I fly back to base."

He took the trouble to learn the name of his opponent in the duel: Lieutenant C. R. Maasdorp, of Ontario, Canada. It was a name he never forgot.

During that fight, and again in combat the next day, he felt a roaring in his ears and a pain like the stab of a hot needle. When he left his plane and walked across the field the Baron noticed him totter with pain and fatigue, and ordered him to go on leave.

Back home in Munich the doctor was grave. "Your flying days are over, young fellow," he said. "The eardrum is badly damaged and the whole middle ear infected."

It was a shock to hear it, but Udet automatically discounted the part about no more flying. While he lived, he would fly—doctor or no doctor.

There was, of course, a joyous reunion with his parents and with his girl Eleanor, whom he called "Lo." Also, there came a telegram from the squadron informing him that he had been awarded the *Pour le Mérite,* which, despite its French name, was Germany's highest combat decoration. However, one evening the newspapers carried the news that Baron von Richthofen, the great Red Knight, had fallen, killed in battle.

Ignoring the protests of his doctor, Udet returned to the front.

The air war had taken on new dimensions. Now the Allies were coming over in formations of 50 planes at a time, and sometimes 100. There was still sufficient scope for the ace to operate on his own, but his day was passing in favor of unit tactics, of co-ordi-

Ernst Udet, stunt pilot: This picture of Udet was taken in 1931 at the Cleveland National Air Races where he thrilled the crowd by doing things, according to a Cleveland reporter, "which no living man should have been able to do." He flew a ship he designed, the U-12 Flamingo.

Acme

nated maneuver, of squadron against squadron. To the last Udet preferred his role as a lone hunter to that of flight leader.

Now he seemed bent on stemming the rising Allied tide singlehanded. His score of kills again began to mount spectacularly. His flamboyant Fokker with "Lo!" painted on its side, next to the Black Cross of Imperial Germany, and with the two streamers of a flight leader, became a scarlet comet up and down the front, a flaming inspiration to his fellow pilots and a flaming menace to Allied airmen.

He did not always escape unscathed, and more than once nothing but his seemingly supernatural luck saved him.

Over the forest of Villers-Cotterets a French observation plane was directing artillery fire, with devastating effect against the German positions. An emergency call from the trenches brought Udet to the scene, and he found the enemy to be a two-seater Bréguet.

In the Bréguet, the observer sat behind the pilot so that when the ship was attacked directly from behind and on the same level the rear machine gun was temporarily useless. If it fired it was in danger of hitting its own tail assembly.

Udet used this approach, aiming his first bursts at the observer. He saw the man's head abruptly disappear below the rim of the cockpit, and assumed he was hit and probably dead.

The pilot of the Bréguet, however, turned out to be a cool and canny flyer, and whisked his heavy plane away in evasive action. Udet decided to attack from the side in order to hit either the pilot or the motor—a maneuver that would be foolish if the observer were in action and able to protect the flank.

Udet came boring in without a qualm and was only 20 meters from the Bréguet when the observer suddenly popped up in the cock-

Another postwar photo of Udet taken when he was attempting to obtain backing for a transatlantic flight. Shortly after this, he made a widely publicized attempt to rescue Gen. Umberto Nobile from the ice floes north of Spitsbergen in 1928.

pit and began working his gun. Under the circumstances, he couldn't miss and he didn't. Udet's plane was riddled.

The control cables had been severed, and the plane began to fly crazily by itself in wide, erratic swoops. Whenever it swung to the east, Udet desperately gave it gas in the hope of urging it to the German side of the lines. But then it nosed over and plummeted straight down toward No Man's Land where the earth was heaving under incessant artillery explosions.

Udet pulled up his legs and stood on the seat, preparing to use his parachute. The slipstream yanked him out and back and smashed him into the tail. The parachute harness, which had been donned in haste, was loose and snagged on the stabilizer. He was caught and held there, a prisoner of the plunging plane.

All the time he was fumbling frantically with the harness where it was caught on the stabilizer, trying to work himself loose. Then, with a sudden, miraculous lurch he was free of the plane and falling alone in the air. At 80 meters up he felt another violent jerk. The parachute opened and he drifted to the churning earth.

He finally reached a German trench and was passed back through the lines to safety. Later that day he flew over the area where his Fokker went down, and spotted it among the shell holes. Before returning to base he shot down a Spad.

His score reached 50, and he received a personal telegram of congratulations from Kaiser Wilhelm II, the Emperor of Germany. He was given the rank of *Oberleutnant* —first lieutenant—by a special royal Prussian order.

J.G. 1 had a new commander, a first lieutenant who arrived with a score of 21 kills. It was a respectable number but by no means awesome. No one could possibly have supplanted the Baron in the esteem of his pilots, but the newcomer fell short by miles. His name was Hermann Goering.

By now there were five Allied planes in the air for every German, and the war was straining toward its climax. As early as August 1918 the word had secretly been given by the high command to the German government in Berlin that the war was lost.

But it went on as bloodily as ever until November, and Udet kept flying and killing to the end. *J.G. 1* was based at Metz when he took off for his last combat flight in World War I.

He led his *Staffel* of six planes against seven De Havilland 9s, two-seater bombers. The fight was more unequal than the numbers indicated because the German planes were all manned by battle-tested veterans with at least two years of experience, while the D.H. 9s were piloted by fledgling Americans. In a melee that lasted less than five minutes, Udet

Wanamaker and Udet, postwar: Thirteen years after he shot him down, Udet (right) returned to Judge Wanamaker the souvenir he had cut from the American's Nieuport. The meeting took place at the Cleveland Air Races, Sept. 6, 1931.

and his flight shot down three of the attacking planes and scattered the formation.

As the Americans dispersed, one of them made the tactical error of flying over Udet's plane. Udet stood his Fokker on its tail and fired straight up. The D.H. crossed his line of fire and exploded, and he had to fall away to the side to avoid the burning wreckage as it came down. That was his second kill for the day.

But the leader of the American flight had returned to the attack, and with his first burst Udet felt a scorching pain in his upper thigh and a spray of gasoline in his face. He and his gas tank had been hit simultaneously. He cut the motor and made a dead-stick landing.

He was helped out of his machine and limped away bleeding to make his last report:

"Sixty-first and sixty-second enemy planes destroyed. . . ."

Ernst Udet had come a long way since his abject failure with his first Caudron. His record was one of the great combat feats of the war on either side.

When the Richthofen *Jagdgeschwader* formally surrendered its planes after the signing of the Armistice, its members returned to a Germany where aviation had come to a complete standstill. To Ernst Udet, greatest of the surviving German aces, a life without flying was unthinkable.

Many years later he was to again become involved in military aviation as first a colonel and then a brigadier general in charge of technical development for the German *Luftwaffe*. While he detested the strutting, stiff-necked Nazis, he was a German patriot who, as a passionate flyer, was naturally enthusiastic about the rebirth of German air power.

Udet was to be primarily responsible for introducing the dive bomber with the screaming siren with which Hitler terrorized Europe during the early days of World War II. He was to fly from factory to factory all over Germany, inspecting new models under construction, test-flying them and making suggestions for further improvements. Then, under pressure after Germany's defeat in the Battle of Britain and from the enemies he had made within the Nazi Party, he was to commit suicide in July 1941 after being taken into custody by the Gestapo.

But these far-reaching events belong to another era. Udet's great passion was flying.

After the Armistice ended World War I, Udet took to the air again as a barnstorming stunt flyer, doing dives, barrel rolls and loops wherever a crowd could be gathered and a collection taken. He stunted at night in the glare of searchlights, and he chased free balloons around the sky. It was only show-off acrobatics in a carnival spirit, but it required the utmost in skill, precision and nerve.

In 1931 he was invited to come to the United States and participate in the National Air Races at Cleveland.

"He did things," wrote one awe-struck Cleveland reporter, "which no living man should have been able to do." He kissed the ground lightly with his wheels, like a ballerina dancing on her toes. He rolled, looped and banked so close to the grandstand that spectators could not only plainly see him in the cockpit but actually read the expression on his face. To the average onlooker it was thrilling enough, but to other flyers who understood the factors of skill, control and audacity involved it was phenomenal.

As a climax Udet brought his motorless ship gracefully to rest on the exact spot from which he had taken off.

A hundred thousand people cheered and stamped and yelled and waved their handkerchiefs as he climbed down from the plane.

They herded him onto the speaker's platform and put him before a microphone with Captain Eddie Rickenbacker, America's greatest wartime ace. Captain Rickenbacker welcomed Udet to America and they saluted each other handsomely as gallant foes.

Udet had come prepared for the next part of the ceremony. The man now mounting the platform was a common pleas judge of Akron, Ohio, named Walter B. Wanamaker—the same Lieutenant Wanamaker Udet had shot down over Château-Thierry in 1918. It was the dramatic highlight of the air races when the two men warmly shook hands: the American grinning amiably at the German who had almost killed him.

Udet added a flourish of his own by reaching into a pocket and pulling out the piece of fabric he had cut from Wanamaker's wrecked Nieuport. "This has the identification number of your plane on it," he said. "I've kept it all these years. Now I want you to have it back." And he handed it over. •

William Barker
Greatest Pilot the World Has Known

By William W. Walker

IN HIS autobiography *Winged Peace*, Billy Bishop, the most famous of Canadian aces, paid Bill (William G.) Barker the ultimate accolade when he labeled him "the greatest fighter pilot the world has ever known."

Was this just one Canadian going overboard on the ability of a fellow countryman? If Barker deserved Bishop's appellation of "greatest" why is he almost unheard of today?

Barker seemed to shun publicity about himself and his exploits. He left no memoirs, in contrast to many of the aces who meticulously set down their autobiographies. There are no known definitive biographies of him and even the R.C.A.F. Air Ministry at Ottawa has only the barest history of one of their most illustrious warriors of World War I. Perhaps the reason that there is only fragmentary information about Barker stems from the fact that he had very little use for system and no patience with protocol. His job was fighting—killing Germans—and it was an employment he pursued with relentless, wholehearted enthusiasm. He lived for the thrill of the chase . . . of combat . . . the final, blazing minute of the kill which was the payoff, the *raison d'être* of the fighter pilot. Each victory spurred him on to new goals, and in the air he was as courageous and reckless as any of the young hellions skimming the clouds over France and Germany.

WILLIAM BARKER

Out of the cockpit, however, he seemed more withdrawn. Somber, reserved, he was different from his more lively compatriots who liked all the carousing and wenching they could crowd into the short hours between flights. Death would join them in the cockpit soon enough, most of them reasoned, so why not live it up?

As a squadron commander, Barker was always concerned with his charges and anxious to teach them the combat tactics that would enable them to survive. He could, when occasion demanded, celebrate and drink with them, but unbridled celebrations and uninhibited acts, so typical of the flying Galahads, just didn't fit in with his personality. Compared with some of the more flamboyant young blades like Lufbery, Udet and Frank Luke, Barker was quite restrained, on the ground at least.

Barker's blunt, laconic speech was in the Gary Cooper tradition and this caused much consternation when his superior officers tried to discipline him.

Puzzled about how to control this young hothead, yet recognizing his remarkable ability, the top brass solved the problem by shipping him off to the secondary Austrian front. This, more than anything else, was probably responsible for the fact that Barker's fame did not measure up to the other World War I greats.

Although Barker got in his initial combat victories over France, he spent most of his time fighting the Austrians in the Italian campaign. Bishop, conversely, piled up his great record on the French and German front. The dreary campaign over the Italian Alps did not receive anywhere near the day-by-day press coverage accorded the main battle theater. Historians and present-day chroniclers have almost forgotten that Italy was allied with the Western Powers against Austria and Germany.

How does Barker rate when compared to René Fonck, Manfred von Richthofen, Georges Guynemer, Micky Mannock or Ernst Udet?

Barker's score of 53 wasn't the highest, but he pioneered fighter pilot tactics that were widely used in World War II and blueprinted a plan for fighter armament that was used by the British in the Battle of Britain in 1940. Few airmen have left such a legacy.

Born on November 3, 1894 Barker grew up in the midwestern prairie land of Manitoba with a keen love for outdoor life. His youthful hunting experience in flushing small game out of the Manitoba bushland made him a superb marksman.

In the summer of 1914 the legions of the Czar and the Kaiser were flexing their muscles and getting ready to march; France and England were mobilizing. When Britain declared war, men from all over the Dominion scrambled to answer the call to arms. In their boiling patriotism many of them, Barker included, feared the fighting would be all over before they could cut red tape and get overseas.

Barker enlisted in the Canadian Army and was sent to Camp Valcartiers. Training at this pioneer boot camp was confused, rugged and exciting. There was plenty of arduous work—long, tiring marches, trench digging, close-order drill, hours on the rifle range, all of the other myriad, menial chores that instill discipline and purpose into raw recruits.

When Barker shipped overseas, he was a member of his Majesty's Canadian Mounted

Lt. Col. William G. Barker, V.C., D.S.O. and Bar, M.C. and two Bars, *Croix de Guerre*, the Italian *Valore Militare*. Veteran of reconnaissance, artillery contact and bombing squadrons, Barker became one of the greatest fighter pilots, was decorated on both French and Italian fronts.
Royal Canadian Air Force

Rifles assigned to a machine gun section with several hundred seasick horses as traveling companions. His regiment reached England in the spring of 1915, and from there they journeyed to France, landing in a dreary, bone-chilling rain.

Bogged down for weeks in the slimiest mud he'd ever seen, Barker almost despaired of ever seeing anything but quagmire, baled hay and the messy end of a horse. He ruefully decided there was nothing glamorous in being a private in the cavalry.

One rainy afternoon a means of delivery from the all-engulfing ocean of mud sputtered down out of the overcast sky. A small Blériot monoplane, its sewing-machine engine crackling, circled the quaggy and bumped to a touchdown near the cavalry encampment. Fascinated and envious, the mud-encrusted young private then and there resolved to transfer.

Barker applied at once for training with the Royal Flying Corps and his request was quickly approved. He was posted to Squadron 9 at Allonville with the rank of corporal for training as an aerial observer.

Manning the rear cockpit of a lumbering, ancient B.E. 2c observation plane on recon flights didn't offer many chances for glory, but it was a vast improvement over the trenches. And it took this spirited young Canuck only a few flights to show his aptitude for air fighting.

One balmy afternoon while returning from a long artillery spotting flight over enemy lines during the battle of Neuve-Chapelle early in March 1916, Barker and his pilot were jumped by a Fokker, the deadliest plane in the air at that phase of the war. In a straight run the slow two-seater didn't have a ghost of a chance of losing the swift fighter.

Barker pivoted his Scarff-mounted Lewis gun and waited patiently as the Fokker closed in for what the Hun pilot thought would be an easy kill. Then Barker cut loose with short, rapid bursts that literally butchered the small fighter. The Fokker nosed up, stalled and started to plummet to earth, its engine pouring out a cloud of oily, black smoke.

This initial taste of blood against superior odds acted like a spur. It also brought immediate action from higher echelons where gunners of this breed were appreciated.

On April 2, 1916 Barker was gazetted as a second lieutenant and sent to No. 4 Squadron on the Somme sector as an observer. He soon became the most unpopular observer in the sector because he kept urging his pilots to fly down lower. This habit of Barker's soon was a subject for heated and vehement discussion when the pilots gathered around the officer's bar.

"Barker, you're crazy, asking us to fly so damn low," one weary pilot complained as he tried to relax with a double whiskey.

"How the hell are you going to see what's going on down there if you don't fly low?" replied Barker. "That's where all the action is—down there on the ground. What good does it do you to plow around up there in the clouds? Might as well bury your head in the mud!"

"The trouble is," chimed in another flyer, "you'll get yourself killed if you keep up those tactics. Why do you have to take some poor bloke of a pilot with you?"

And while Barker's "chauffeurs" groused and grumbled because he wanted to mix in the middle of ground action, men in headquarters were impressed. Barker was soon sent for pilot training. He breezed through ground school with consummate ease and teachers tabbed him as a "comer," forgetting, perhaps, his baptism by fire in the rear cockpit. He knew every square inch of the crates he'd flown in and his reflexes were lightning quick.

The fact that he soloed after exactly one hour of dual stick time was proof of his splendid natural co-ordination and inherent ability. Barker's instructor sensed that his confident, clear-eyed cadet was no heavy-handed fledgling who would take weeks or months to grasp the feel of the stick. He put Barker through a complete routine—right and left turns that mounted each time in steepness of angle; gliding turns to port and starboard, corkscrew spins, power-off stalls, loops and banks around crude pylons—enough dizzying maneuvers to make the average bloke wish he'd never left the infantry.

Whatever teacher did, pupil repeated just as well. When they landed, the instructor unfastened his belt, left the motor running and climbed out, shaking his head as though he didn't believe what he was about to say.

"Barker, it's a cinch you're no Quirk (an unskilled flight student). As far as I'm concerned, you're bloody well ready to be kicked out of the nest. Go on. Take it around yourself."

Without further ado, Billy maneuvered the biplane down the runway, gently nudged his rudder as gentle play with throttle and stick surged the trainer ahead and off the field. Barker repeated the pattern of tricks and exercises, and when he landed and taxied up the flight line, his instructor was waiting.

"Barker, I've got to hand it to you," the other said. "You're either completely mad or a born flying genius. Maybe you're both."

When Barker returned to France in January 1917 as a pilot, he was posted to No. 15 Squadron as a flight commander. This meant flying the slow, clumsy observation crate, the R. E. 8. Again he chafed at the bit. How could you do any damage to the German Air Service in those old planes? Once again his squawking caught the attention of the brass—but this time the results were not good.

The brass who noticed him were so impressed by the way he flew the awkward observation planes that they sent him back to England as an instructor.

It didn't take the restless young pilot long to get completely bored with the humdrum atmosphere of a training squadron. Teaching fledglings to fly was just not his cup of tea. But though he begged to be returned to combat duty he was turned down cold.

Barker listened to the refusals—but he didn't hear them. He was going to get back to the front—one way or the other.

The first way he chose was the right one. He began buzzing sleepy rural villages, frightening farmers and livestock into near panic as he scraped his wheels on every roof top in sight. He snap-rolled his Camel upside down under every bridge from Southampton to London, raising havoc with the peaceful river traffic. "Blimey, 'ere comes that lunatic again," the boatmen would shout as they ducked for cover.

When he buzzed headquarters, it was at chimney level, and he flew so low he virtually left rubber tread marks on the shingle roofs. This was one of Barker's favorite tricks and became his trade-mark. Repeatedly he was hauled up on the official carpet, reamed out and ordered to mend his erratic flying manners.

Finally, after a monumental chewing out by an exasperated squadron commander, Barker took his Camel up and staged a show that had veteran pilots reaching for the nearest bottle. First he nosed his maneuverable Sopwith up in the sharpest climbing turn that particular field had ever seen. When he flattened out of his abrupt climb, he wavered as though he would stall out and spin in, nose first. But he didn't stall. He flipped over in a fast roll and zoomed straight for a cluster of pilots who scattered in panic. In complete mastery of his machine, he pulled the nose up and cleared a hangar roof with feet to spare. Next came a succession of snap rolls—100 feet off the ground.

The next mad maneuver was a run at full speed between two hangars. On the return trip Barker dropped the Camel's nose into a vertical dive, pulled up, leveled off and then

Barker beside his Sopwith Camel on the drome of 28 Squadron, R.F.C., Italian front. The Sopwith Camel was Barker's favorite ship. When he was made commander of a Bristol Fighter squadron he led the Bristols into combat in his trustworthy Camel.

Imperial War Museum

sidcslipped gently in a falling leaf that put him in position for a perfect landing.

Five minutes after he landed, he was on the carpet again.

"Barker," roared the commanding officer, "what in blazes are we going to do with you? I'm getting damned tired of chewing you out day after day. You're going to kill yourself and some innocent parties in the bargain if you don't stop this clowning. Do we have to court-martial you to make you obey orders?"

"No, sir," replied Barker, "just let me go back to combat. I joined up to kill Germans, not to teach rookies. Next time I might buzz the Tower of London. I'll get back to France if I have to fracture every rule in the book."

For the first time, this familiar scene had the ending Barker wanted. And when he returned to the front, it was as commander of a flight in No. 28 Squadron. For this tour of combat he was to fly a Sopwith Camel, the plane he had already mastered in his bridge-buzzing antics—the plane Billy Bishop described as "that delicate piece of sudden death."

Barker was a master of sky tactics, and had what one expert described as "telescopic eyes that searched for prey like some questing eagle." He could discern the faintest speck, even when half hidden by clouds, and this, of course, proved an overwhelming advantage in combat when position and surprise meant the difference between victory or death.

A superb gunner, equaled perhaps only by Bishop and René Fonck, he was frugal with his ammo, preferring to finish the enemy with short, lethal bursts at 20 to 30 yards. Before taking off, he'd check his guns and links round by round, pulling them through the breech with all the loving care of a master gunnery sergeant.

Albert Ball, idol of every R.F.C. pilot, had crashed to his death in May 1917, and all the young aces who were trying to pass his score, Micky Mannock, Billy Bishop, James McCudden, now were fighting for the honor and

glory of being Britain's top fighter pilot. Barker, too, had this ambition.

Flying every day weather permitted, he was always looking for a fight.

Some of the pent-up frustration he had choked back as a two-seater pilot came exploding to the surface when he scored his initial double kill, smashing two Halberstadt scouts.

One day, while on a solo flight over Vimy Ridge, he found seven red Halberstadt scouts deployed in formation below him. Using a protective cloud cover as a shield, he closed in like a big game stalker and nailed the trailing Hun from 30 yards away with one deadly spray of tracer. Zooming abruptly as the crimson German fighter exploded into a swirling mass of debris, Barker barged back into the startled formation and nailed his second victim, another flamer. The rest of the Huns scattered, leaving the exuberant Canadian all to himself.

In less than five minutes of deadly, concentrated pinpoint shooting he had raised hell with a superior enemy formation.

It was a fitting way to celebrate his return to combat and when he approached his field, he let off some more steam by splitessing all over the drome, then buzzing the hangars before coming in for a perfect landing.

In a letter home, he described his baptism by fire in the agile Sopwith Camel as "... really great sport—the most fun I ever had. Perhaps it sounds bloodthirsty, but I have never enjoyed myself so much as I did this afternoon, beating odds of seven to one."

The Camel was powered by a 130-horsepower Clerget motor that rotated at 1,250 revolutions per minute with the prop. The crankshaft was bolted to the air frame and all other components—cylinders, pistons, crankcase—turned with the prop. This whirlwind of weight, spinning as it did, set up a deadly torque. Some observers swore the Camel killed as many novices as it did Germans—and it officially accounted for 1,634 German planes, some balloons and one Zeppelin. The gyroscopic torque of the Clerget inclined the Camel to enter an outside loop when dived vertically, and many a pilot found himself in inverted flight with no means of support as his wings peeled off.

Seasoned pilots, though, loved the Camel for its superior maneuverability. No German plane ever built could follow the elusive product of Mr. T. O. M. Sopwith through a right turn, and men like Barker were quick to drive the Germans crazy—and into the ground—by fighting down at low altitudes. It was a fearsome ground strafer, dreaded by the German infantry, and it was far too elusive for "Archy" to blast out of the sky.

Barker was idolized by his mechanics and ground crew, and although officers and enlisted men, by normal protocol, didn't share the same mess hall or drink together, Barker's ground crew considered it a challenge to indulge in friendly wassail with him when he celebrated a victory.

As his skill developed Barker perfected new fighter tactics. One favorite was the trick of luring his foes into battle as close to the ground as possible, so that he could utilize the superior agility of the Camel.

He first put his system to an acid test one day at twilight as he led his flight home from a strafing foray against German troops massing on the Ypres-Menin road, deep behind enemy lines.

Suddenly ten black-crossed Albatroses loomed up in the dusk, heading east for home. Barker dipped his wings and his mates peeled off in attack. The scrap was barely under way when Barker, trying to assist one of his formation, found a Hun moving into position on his tail.

Zigzagging to keep just out of range, he circled lower and lower to the ground, making no effort to get into shooting position, luring the German right down to the tree tops.

Suddenly he executed a tight loop with his responsive Camel, and in a split second was on his foe's tail. One accurate burst ended the fight. A second Hun pounced on him seeking to avenge his fallen friend. Barker repeated the maneuver—with the same result.

Headquarters took careful note of Barker's roof-top tactics and dogfighting strategy. The top brass were so impressed with his skill that they decided to form a squadron of men like Barker—reckless, high-spirited young pilots who were fearless enough and headstrong enough to be trained in this wild

Canadian's system. After the unit was organized, it was shipped to Italy to fight the Germans and Austrians in the mountain passes where they were threatening to overwhelm the Italian Army. A massive attack at Caporetto in October 1917 by Austro-German forces had broken the Italian front, and their rout of the Italians was primarily due to their complete mastery of the air. Austrian and German reconnaissance planes had prepared photographic maps of the entire front virtually unmolested by Italian planes.

The appearance on the Italian front of three R.F.C. squadrons, including Barker's Squadron 28, along with fresh British and French troops, soon changed the tide of war.

Shortly after their arrival on the scene, a routine patrol of Barker's Camels discovered a massive concentration of troops and artillery starting over the Piave River bridge and the three R.F.C. units bombed and strafed for two days until the surprise assault became a bloody rout.

That was the beginning of an orgy. Now the youngsters ran amuck, blowing hitherto unmolested Austrian *Drachen* (observation balloons) out of the skies far behind enemy lines, bombing supply depots and strafing railroad marshaling yards.

But it was the boss man himself, Barker, who staged the most spectacular raid of the war on that front—on Christmas Day of 1917.

No patrols were scheduled for the holiday. Barker and several of his squadron mates waited impatiently for dinner, restless and bored, unable to summon up any holiday spirit in their drab surroundings. Within easy viewing distance they could see an Austrian balloon swinging lazily in the chill afternoon light, its steel cables winding down like tentacles to motor-driven winches.

"Say, what do you think we ought to do about that insolent beggar over there spying down our backs?" Barker asked.

"The Italians made a go at it the other day, but ground crew reeled it in too damn fast," Captain Cliff answered.

"Well, why don't we make a stab at it anyway? It would make a real nice Christmas surprise for the Colonel," mused Barker. "I'll hug those hills and, Riley and Cliff, you ride top cover for me just in case."

Moments later they were air-borne. Barker, flying low and in the fastest Camel, took the balloon and its crew completely by surprise. He finished the *Drachen* with two bursts of incendiary fire.

As he pulled up, he spotted an Austrian airdrome nearby. He signaled his two companions, who hadn't fired a burst, and zoomed

The Bristol Fighter was the greatest fighting ship in Italy and one of the greatest of the war. In July 1918 Barker was promoted to major and given command of 139 Squadron with two flights of Bristols. Despite his preference for the Camel, Barker sometimes flew a Bristol, and on one occasion had Edward, Prince of Wales, along on a flight over the Austrian lines as his gunner-observer.

Bristol Aeroplane Company Ltd.

straight down for the wide open hangar doors. His wheels scraped the tarmac, and as he pulled up, his twin machine guns tore up a row of parked planes. He zoomed up and over the hangar, his squadron mates close behind.

Rudely jolted out of their Christmas reverie, the Austrians came to life with machine guns blazing from every corner. Barker and his flight repeated the strafing pattern on the second hangar and finished off the third shed, leaving it a blazing inferno. Then, gun to gun, wing to wing, the three Canucks wheeled and fought with the entrenched defenders until their ammo drums clattered, empty.

When the three marauders finally headed for home, they left in their wake three hangars reduced to smoldering ashes, 15 planes ruined and 13 Austrians dead.

German squadrons sent in to assist the harassed Austrians decided to pay Barker and his young lunatics a visit. Thirty huge, heavily armed Gotha bombers were dispatched to obliterate the Allied drome. The "lesson" backfired when Barker and his squadron roared into battle with new tactics and strategy that knocked half of the intruders out of the sky.

The Canadians used the head-on approach —an approach that took iron nerves. To nail your man you flew a collision course straight at him, on his level, pouring on the gas and holding back on the trigger until somebody weakened.

That's how Barker dealt with the Gothas taking three out of three in his first encounter.

The three huge bombers were flying in line when Billy barged into them head-on. He nailed the first when they were almost bow to bow, zoomed under the second, stitching the pilot's compartment with a deadly spray of lead, then leveled off at point blank range into the third, edged it out of formation and knocked it down in a vortex of oily flames.

Thus ended 1917 for the wild young Canadian who had been in uniform since hostilities started in 1914. In January 1918 he added seven more Austrians to his total and brought his bag to 15.

What aided Barker so much at this time was the fact he was a master tactician, who could anticipate situations. The way he knocked down everything the Germans could get off a tarmac, from Fokker Dreideckers to Halberstadts to Gothas, whether over France or Italy and be it a formation of ten planes or 60, proved that this flying dervish knew his business. He knew it from hard experience in the back seat of ungainly observation planes, from long, frustrating months flying slow recon planes and by the tactics that bore the "Made by Barker" trade-mark. He knew and loved his ships, from ammunition belts to wing struts, from the tail skid to the woodenbladed prop up front.

Barker continued to improve his low flying tactics, always preferring this method to conventional strategy of getting between the enemy and the sun and then pouncing. He wanted them down scraping their undercarriage on the shrubbery, but to find them this low he had to visit their fields and lie in

The Caproni, Italy's great bomber, staged many raids over the Alps and into Austrian territory, often escorted by Barker and his Bristols.

*There were actually four Austrians referred to in the challenge, the names being somewhat garbled. They were Goodwin Brumowski, Benno Fiala, Ritter von Fernbrugg and Friedrich Navratil.

ambush. His system worked like a charm, and enemy planes were swatted down like house flies. Barker's tunic soon sagged from the sheer weight of the decorations that came his way. The Distinguished Service Order was added to the Military Cross he won as an observer, then came a Bar to the D.S.O., a Bar to the M.C., plus medals from the grateful Italians.

Other honors came his way in 1918. After transferring for a short time to 66 Squadron, he was promoted to major in July and given command of 139 Squadron. Just prior to this, legend relates that he scored his great victory over Linke-Crawford.

"Captain" Linke-Crawford, the top Austrian pilot, had become the deadliest scourge on that sector, with 23 kills—and had become the man Barker had to get.

When he finally tangled with him one afternoon, Barker, for the first time, feared he had more than met his match. The Austrian and his tiny ship outmaneuvered him and his Camel with consummate ease, and on three separate occasions was in a killing position. Crawford, a master flyer and clever strategist, fortunately was a lousy shot.

Realizing he couldn't outmaneuver Crawford, Barker took a gambler's chance. Wheeling out of his tight situation he flew head-on for Crawford. For several tense, agonizing seconds the two antagonists threw a barrage of lead at each other. Then the wily Austrian, noting that he was being outshot, dropped his nose and pulled out of the collision course. This was exactly what Barker expected. With split-second precision, he dropped on the Austrian and shot him down in flames. Crawford slumped convulsively in his cockpit and crashed on the very edge of his field.

Now Billy and some of his comrades tried to lure the next three top Austrian pilots into battle, but with little luck. This trio would consistently streak for home whenever the Canadians in their scrappy Camels appeared on the scene. To taunt the enemy into doing battle, Barker had thousands of leaflets printed with the following challenge, and dropped them at enemy airdromes:

> *Major William G. Barker, D.S.O., M.C., and the officers under his command, present their compliments to*
> *Captain Brumowsky,*
> *Rither von Fiala,*
> *Captain Havratil,*
> *and the pilots under their command and request the pleasure and the honor of meeting them in the air. In order to save Captain Brumowsky, Rither von Fiala and Captain Havratil and the Gentlemen of their party the inconvenience of searching for them, Major Barker and his officers will bomb Godega Airdrome at 10:00 a.m. daily, weather permitting, for the ensuing fortnight.**

Barker and his young firebrands carried out their schedule to the very moment. They bombed and strafed Godega day after day. Once or twice enemy planes appeared as a face-saving gesture, but, as always, Barker and

U. S. Signal Corps

his group came out on top by a lopsided score.

Enemy fliers weren't the only men cursing Barker at this time. Joining in the hate chorus was a horde of Allied spies. Late in 1917 it became common practice to drop Allied spies by parachute. Very few people knew anything about this new device, and the spies themselves didn't enthusiastically endorse the idea of dangling under a flimsy silk umbrella in the blackness of night. Many an agent, setting out on his dangerous mission, would get cold feet and decide not to jump when he reached the appointed spot over his destination. After several frustrating experiences with secret agents who changed their minds at the last minute, Barker set about to remedy the situation.

He secretly equipped the rear seat with a crude trap door operated by a lever in the pilot's cockpit. The passenger, of course, was kept in blissful ignorance. During the flight Barker would reassure his nervous passenger that everything was going along fine, then when the appointed rendezvous behind the Austrian lines was reached, he would spring the trap. The shivering spy died a thousand deaths as he waited for his chute to open. Since each passenger traveled on a one-way ticket, it was easy to keep the secret from future passengers, and the intelligence staff was delighted at such satisfactory delivery service.

By September 1918 Barker's score stood at 47 confirmed victories. But he was finding it difficult to add to his total. The Austrian and German airmen, aware of his deadly reputation, simply refused to fight.

It was then that Barker's superiors were struck with another incongruous idea. He was ordered back to England to teach, of all things, air fighting tactics. It was indeed ironic; a man going back to school to teach from the very book he was busy writing. His head-on style of attack was widely used a

Royal Air Force

GREATEST PILOT THE WORLD HAS KNOWN

generation later in World War II, as was his low level strategy.

Again Barker rebelled. This time he argued that he should have a fortnight in France to acquaint himself with new German planes and tactics. He won his argument and was sent to 201 Squadron.

On October 27 he rang down the curtain on a magnificent career, playing the starring role in the most astounding and dramatic air battle of the entire war.

He had no business mixing in a dogfight that day. He'd packed his gear and shipped it to England. When he climbed into his new Sopwith Snipe, he should have headed straight over the English Channel to Hounslow. But he went far out of his way looking for trouble, and he found a whole hornet's nest of snarling Boche fighters to fade his bet.

He spotted a German two-seater, flying along at 20,000 feet well over its own lines, serene in the belief that no British plane could possibly bother him. Barker poured

In the Sopwith Snipe (left), one of the finest airplanes of the war, Barker fought singlehanded against 60 German aircraft. Although badly wounded, he miraculously escaped with his life. The Snipe appeared late, in Sept. 1918.

This formal portrait of Lt. Col. William G. Barker in full regimentals was taken before the presentation of the Victoria Cross at Buckingham Palace for his epic dogfight of Oct. 27.
Royal Canadian Air Force

the throttle to the Snipe and attacked. When the Hun observer searching the blank sky for the whining Snipe finally found the range, the Canadian was a scant 30 yards away. But the rear seat gunner swiveled his Scarff-mounted Spandaus accurately and Barker's Snipe was badly riddled.

Barker was now fighting under a handicap. His telescopic sight had been stripped off for the homeward flight, so now he was aiming through ordinary peep sights. On his third pass he killed the observer, pulled up under the Albatros and fired a line of flaming tracers into the Hun's fuel tank. A tiny bud of flame quickly roared into a blazing inferno as Barker pulled his tiny fighter away just in time. The German plane exploded.

A nearby Fokker triplane joined the melee, catching Barker by surprise. An explosive bullet shattered his right hip, but he wheeled on the triplane and knocked it down in flames.

Struggling to remain conscious, Barker looked around to get his bearings and found himself the center of a swirling maelstrom of more than 60 German scouts rushing up to avenge the Fokker. He sensed he was in his last fight. Hit repeatedly, he fainted from loss of blood when a bullet smashed his left thigh. The Snipe, spinning dizzily out of control, fell thousands of feet with the whole German circus in pursuit.

As the rush of air revived him, he turned on his assailants like a snarling animal at bay. He had put out of his pain-fatigued mind any hope of survival, and charged the nearest German head-on, hoping to take at least one more with him.

They barely missed colliding and the Fokker dove straight into the ground. Barker's left elbow was now hanging limp and useless, shattered by another explosive bullet. He blacked out again—then recovered and quickly sent three more Germans spinning out of control or in flames.

Stifling his agony by sheer will power, fighting to keep from blacking out again, Barker leveled his decimated Sopwith and picked out the nearest target, a speedy Fokker D-7. As the first slugs ricocheted off his motor cowling, the German panicked, tried to dive and outrace the tenacious banshee on his tail. It was a final, fatal mistake. Barker corrected his aim and sent a spray of lead into the cockpit.

Barker nailed two more Fokkers before a burst of explosive bullets perforated the fuel tank under his seat. Inexplicably, for self-sealing gas tanks were unknown then, the Snipe didn't catch fire. Fighting to keep his senses, Barker switched to his auxiliary tank and kept the Clerget engine going. Again he fainted and almost spun into the ground, recovering just in time to pull out. His tiny ship whirling like a leaf in a windstorm, Barker headed west and barely managed to somersault into a barbed-wire entanglement just inside British lines.

A company of Scottish troops, fascinated spectators of the epic dogfight, pulled the unconscious pilot from the wreckage.

In a complete coma for two weeks in a base hospital at Rouen, Barker's vitality and sheer will to live pulled him through.

On November 30 he was awarded the Victoria Cross for that climactic aerial brawl. Nineteen British and Canadian flyers won the highest honor a British subject could earn, and no one deserved it more than Barker. It was without doubt the most dramatic fight of the war, pitting as it did the Allies' finest fighter against Germany's best, the D-7 and Fokker triplanes. It was also the last great dogfight of World War I. The Armistice ended hostilities two weeks later.

Bill Barker's final tally as a war pilot was 53, but this simple figure covers only the fringe of his greatness. It is claimed for him, and admittedly difficult to prove, that he flew a greater number of hours over the lines than any pilot in the war; he fought the enemy's best in the air on two fronts; he destroyed balloons and bridges; he won decorations as observer and pilot, as two-seater pilot and pursuit pilot; he repeatedly attacked infantry—and that he may have averted a terrible defeat for the Allied Armies in Italy. •

"Greatest Pilot the World Has Known:" William G. Barker with the engine and guns from the Sopwith Snipe in which he fought his great aerial battle against overwhelming odds on Oct. 27, 1918.

Royal Canadian Air Force

Frank Luke
Balloon Buster

By William E. Barrett

THERE are two sides to every man's life, two sets of images that he leaves behind. Finding the real man in a mass of conflicting testimony is a fascinating job.

Frank Luke was, in real life, the ideal hero of a TV western, a reckless, daring fighter who went out in a blaze of glory with a flaming pistol in his hand. He is perfect material for anyone's story of a fearless World War I ace and has been the subject of many such stories. He, seemingly, had everything.

Eddie Rickenbacker has said that, "Luke was the greatest fighter who ever went into the air." Indeed, Luke was second only to Rickenbacker in the roll call of American aces and the only other fighter pilot to win the Congressional Medal of Honor.

On the other hand, one of the pilots who served with him described Luke as "the stupidest guy in the A.E.F., land, sea or air."

The "stupid" remark can be understood only if we remember that Luke specialized in destroying German balloons. And those balloons were protected by rings of antiaircraft and machine guns. Pilots who considered themselves sane wanted no part of them and they looked with suspicion on anyone who specialized in attacking them. Attacking balloons just wasn't reasonable. Luke was the only American pilot who attacked them because he liked to do it.

FRANK LUKE

The whole business of balloons was not normal. Balloon men themselves were considered not quite human; not air service, not infantry, not artillery, not anything that could be classified or understood. A balloon observer sat up in the sky in a jiggling basket under a big swaying gas bag and observed troop movements through binoculars.

He was equipped with a monstrous parachute. Because of his training, he was considered more valuable than the balloon, so he had orders to jump if attacked. He was often attacked, and many of the attackers just feinted to make him jump, but didn't go all the way in for fear of endangering themselves. The primitive parachute of those days set a jumper down hard and bounced him along the ground.

There was a front-line story about a pilot in a French bar telling how he worried a certain German balloonist. "I made a pass at him every time I crossed the lines," he said, "and every time I made a pass, he jumped out of the basket. They always sent him up again, too, the same Kraut. I got so I could recognize him."

A short, stocky individual drinking at one of the tables got up, walked over to the bar, knocked the daring pilot cold with one punch and walked out without saying a word. He was an American balloon observer and he had more in common with the German who had to jump out of the balloon than he had with the American flier who made him jump.

Incidents like that gave the balloon business a bad name and Luke's fame is forever linked to balloons.

Frank Luke the boy was very much like Frank Luke the man. He was born in Phoenix, Arizona, May 19, 1897, long before Phoenix became noted as a rich man's play-

National Archives

Frank Luke as he appeared when he was ferrying planes in France. Since the job gave him no chance to distinguish himself, he tried to impress others with words rather than deeds. Fate stepped in and he was transferred to 27th Aero Squadron.

The challenge that sparked Luke (right): An enemy balloon hanging in the sky ringed by protective, accurately-ranged guns. Until he discovered the challenge of balloons, Luke was worthless to the squadron due to his unreliable, irresponsible behavior. He became greatest destroyer of balloons.

ground. At that time it was merely a small western town—though a fairly tough one.

Frank was of German blood. His father was born in Prussia and had served his compulsory hitch in the German Army. He was a strict man who ruled his large family with a firm hand and Frank, one of nine children, developed early a resentment of discipline, something which marked him all his life.

If he lived in our own day, Luke would probably be the type of character portrayed in teen-age rebel dramas. He did not have a leather jacket or a motorcycle, but he did have a horse and a cowboy outfit. He was a poor student but a star athlete with letters in baseball, football and track, a good swimmer, a crack shot with rifle and pistol and a quick-tempered scrapper. When he was 17 he went into the ring against a touring professional prize fighter named Haney and knocked him out in the first round.

There was swagger in Frank Luke and boastfulness and conceit and temper. He was outstanding in the physical things that interested him most and he never doubted that he would excel in anything else that came along. War came along and he was interested.

On September 25, 1917 in Tucson, Arizona, Frank Luke enlisted as a private in the signal corps requesting flying duty. He was assigned to the school of military aeronautics at Austin, Texas.

Luke was 20 years old. He had 170 pounds distributed over five feet ten inches of lean, hard, wiry body. People who liked him remembered that he had an attractive smile, but his mouth was thin-lipped, straight; the kind of mouth that western writers like to describe. He had gray eyes that did not ordinarily express warmth—the eyes of a hunter, alert and intent but not friendly.

Ground school bored Luke, but because he

U. S. Air Corps

wanted to be a pilot he worked hard. In November 1917 he graduated and was sent to flight training at Rockwell Field in California. He had all of the qualities of a good pilot; keen eyes, good co-ordination, the reflexes of a trained athlete, a horseman's sense of balance, a mind untroubled by imagination, steady nerves. On January 23, 1918 he was commissioned a second lieutenant in the aviation section of the signal corps.

Luke, like so many others, went directly to the aviation instruction center at Issoudun when he landed in France. It was a great mill in which pilots were crushed, killed or shaped into fighting men. Luke saw many of them killed and knew many who washed out. He himself had narrow escapes in the tricky training planes that he flew, but his confidence in himself never wavered.

On May 30, Luke left Issoudun for Cazeaux, the pilot pool from which pilots moved to the front. He was sent to Orly as a ferry pilot flying new ships up to the lines. He disliked his work and resented the fact that he was given no chance to distinguish himself.

At Orly on his ferrying job, Luke came back from a trip when he pleased, flaunted authority, ignored the fact that his independence made more work for other men and excused his own conduct with flamboyant statements that he came over to fight, not ferry.

On July 26, Luke was assigned suddenly and without warning to the 27th Aero Squadron.

Twenty-seven was one of the four squadrons which comprised the First Pursuit Group. The other squadrons were 94, 95 and 147. Major Harold E. Hartney commanded the 27th Squadron and the drome was at Touquin, 25 miles south of Château-Thierry. The squadron was equipped with Spads.

Luke's reputation as a braggart and a malcontent had preceded him and he lost no time in justifying it.

In the mess he showed no respect for older pilots and the squadron record meant nothing to him. He couldn't understand why, with all the time that they had on the front, they were not all aces—and he said so.

On July 31, the First Pursuit Group had its darkest day. All of the squadrons lost men, but the 27th was hardest hit. Flight Leader John McArthur and five of the six men he led were shot down in a fight against odds behind the German lines.

Major Hartney included Luke in a five-man patrol he took out the following day. Luke was told to keep his place in the formation and to watch the leader's signals. Twenty-seven could not afford any more losses.

Luke was not interested in routine squadron patrols, particularly when the patrol was a simple formation flight which bored him. He dropped out after half an hour and went flying off on his own. When the flight returned, Major Hartney was furious.

"Where in hell did you go and why?" he demanded.

National Archives

The older face of Frank Luke: The strain and danger of balloon busting have left their marks on Luke's face as this photograph reveals.

"I had engine trouble."

The answer was obviously false because Luke had flown nearly as long as the patrol, landing only a few minutes ahead of the flight. Hartney, however, preferred not to raise the issue. He explained grimly that other men might have died because the absence of one man left the flight unbalanced. Luke was unimpressed. On the next patrol, he dropped out again. His excuse this time was that he saw a German two-seater and went down after it. None of the veterans who flew with him had seen a two-seater and they did not believe that Luke had either.

After this episode Hartney told him bluntly that he could not risk the lives of other men by burdening the flight with a chronic deserter. He was grounded for a week.

Luke was furious. In the face of the obvious hostility in the mess he retreated into sullen silence. When his suspension was lifted he flew behind Major Hartney again and again dropped out of the formation shortly after the take-off. He did not land until after the flight had returned and this time Major Hartney did not handle him with gloves. Luke listened to the dressing-down with a smile on his face, then interrupted.

"Anyway," he said, "I shot down a Hun."
"The hell you did! Where?"

Luke was vague as to where the combat had occurred, but he supplied a great deal of information about how he had attacked a German flight behind enemy lines and destroyed the rearmost plane. Hartney ordered an investigation of the claim but no confirmation was obtained.

This is one of the most controversial incidents in the Luke career. He had lied before. There was the engine trouble that was never substantiated. He had never had a combat in the air and he had not demonstrated any skill, save his unquestioned flying ability, since joining the squadron. His squadron again branded him a liar and Luke challenged several members to fight.

Lawrence La Tourette Driggs, a journalist assigned to the First Pursuit Group, wrote a book in which he stated that he had read Luke's diary and that in one entry Luke admitted faking his first victory claim.

Whether he lied on that occasion or not, Luke was an outcast in the squadron. No flight commander wanted Luke behind him and no pilot wanted him for a friend. None but Joe Wehner.

Joe Wehner was a steady, courageous pilot with no flair for the spectacular. He was a silent, withdrawn young man who had no close friends. The friendship which he gave generously and wholeheartedly to Frank Luke was Luke's salvation; without it the world would probably have never heard of Luke.

Wehner was from Boston and because he was of German parentage he was investigated by the secret service several times after his enlistment.

After he left Exeter Academy, Joe Wehner volunteered to go to Germany for the Y.M.C.A and work in the prisoner of war camps distributing packages and mail to the British and Americans who were held prisoner. The United States was not at war at the time.

When the U.S. severed diplomatic relations with Germany, Wehner immediately resigned his post and applied for passage home.

The secret service could hardly be blamed for investigating him, for wondering if he had developed strong German sympathies, but Wehner was irreparably hurt by the suspicion. He felt that his comrades in Squadron 27 mistrusted him and he drew into a shell, ignoring friendly overtures, doing his work well but forming no close attachments.

Luke and his predicament interested Wehner. He had known young men like Luke in the prison camps; men with the reckless, egotistical natures which made them ideal soldiers in battle, poor garrison troops and desperate prisoners. He made his first friendly overtures in the squadron to Luke. He encouraged him to talk and he listened to him patiently when no one else would listen at all.

Only when Luke criticized and damned Major Hartney did Wehner stop him. "No," he said. "Hartney is all right. He has been good to you. He could break you and he hasn't."

Wehner was right about that as he was about many things. Hartney *was* good to Luke. Luke was a problem, a thorn in his side and of absolutely no value to the squadron.

FRANK LUKE

The Major discussed Luke with his flight leaders, particularly Jerry Vasconcelles who seemed to understand him best. Neither Hartney nor Vasconcelles believed that Luke had any fear in him.

"It isn't courage exactly," Vasconcelles said. "He has no imagination. He can't imagine anything happening to him. He thinks he's invincible. If he ever finds himself he may be almost as good as he thinks he is."

As a result of that discussion, Hartney permitted Luke to fly solo patrols. It wasn't good for squadron morale and the other pilots did not like it, especially when it seemed that Luke had none of the duties they had. But none of them wanted him in the same flight and there did not seem to be any other answer.

Luke flew. He went out and he crossed the lines and he patrolled by himself and he came back, but he scored no victories.

August marched into September and Luke was still a squadron cipher. On September 3 the squadron moved to Erize-la-petite, 15 miles south of Verdun. Major Hartney was appointed commander of the First Pursuit Group and Captain Al Grant became commander of the 27th. Grant did not approve of babying Frank Luke.

On his flight with Grant, Luke dropped out, landed on the drome of *Les Cigognes*, the famous French Storks, got drunk while trying to impress his hosts and stayed AWOL till next day. Grant grounded him.

When he was restored to duty, Luke repeated the desertion and again visited the Storks.

Wehner tried in vain to plead with him. Grant would have court-martialed him but Hartney, who was fascinated by some strange quality that he saw in Luke, advised further patience. Then on September 11 there was a discussion in the mess that seemed no more momentous than any other, but was destined to have an epochal result. The talk centered on observation balloons. The veteran pilots were agreed that they wanted no part of them, that only on direct order would they attack one.

Jerry Vasconcelles, who was highly respected as one of the finest flight leaders on the front, added his verdict. "I would never order a man down on a balloon," he said. "I'd go down myself before I'd do that, but I'd rather that the issue never came up."

That was the general attitude among men who had tested and knew the hazards of aerial warfare. Balloons were surrounded by antiaircraft guns and the gunners, knowing the exact altitude of the balloon, could shoot above it laying a curtain of fire through which an attacker must dive. Within the ring of antiaircraft guns was another ring of machine guns. Some of the machine gunners ranged their fire to crisscross above the bag while others ranged on either flank where an attacker must swerve after his attack. On an auxiliary field close to the balloon several German pursuit ships were usually in readiness to take off in case of attack.

Luke, sitting on one side of the room with Wehner, listened, fascinated. "I'm going to get one of those balloons," he said. "All those guys are scared of them. I'll show them."

Wehner nodded. He knew Luke's need for vindication, for glory at any cost. "Perhaps you should," he said.

"I'll get one tomorrow if you'll fly upstairs and keep the Fokkers off me."

Wehner flew his regular patrols with the squadron, but he didn't hesitate. "I'll do it," he said.

The following morning, Luke and Wehner took off. They flew to Marieulles where a German balloon strained against its cable. High in the sky they circled, studying it. Luke had no plan. He simply peeled off and dived straight down on the big target.

All of the antiaircraft guns went into action as the Spad dived. Luke flew through a sky that seemed filled with shrapnel and into an area of buzzing machine gun bullets. He fired into the big bag and he held his fire on it, ignoring the death that reached for him through rents and tears in his ship. Suddenly the sky was black with smoke, shot through with flame.

Balloon in flames: This is how a German balloon appeared to Frank Luke when he pulled his Spad up after pouring incendiary Buckingham bullets into it. Balloon busting was a dangerous sport.

The explosion of the balloon tossed the Spad upward like a toy. Luke, still under fire, raced toward his own lines. High above, Wehner patrolled watching his friend, but no Fokkers showed. Luke flew directly to the nearest American observation balloon nest and landed in the auxiliary field.

"Did you see me get that German balloon?" he asked the first officer he saw.

"We sure did. We all did."

Wehner, while Luke was obtaining his confirmation, had gone along on his own, attacked the next balloon in line and blazed it down without anyone upstairs to protect him. His feat almost passed unnoticed because he did not talk about it; he merely entered the required combat report.

Frank Luke had never heard of the other balloon destroyers and he did not even suspect that there were men who specialized in balloon destruction. He had done something that others admittedly avoided and in doing it he had tasted glory for the first time.

"I'm going to get more balloons," he told Captain Grant. "I'm going to get a hell of a lot more balloons."

"Okay." Grant nodded. "There's one at Buzy that corps is complaining about. Somebody in first group was going to draw it out of a hat. If you want it, you can have it."

"I want it. But I want Joe Wehner upstairs."

Luke had Wehner in a flight led by Grant. Arriving over Buzy, Luke dived away from the formation and went down. He headed straight for the bag through the flaming rings, poured his bullets into it in a steady stream and zoomed. The gas bag dissolved into flame behind him as he climbed.

Eight Fokkers came out of the sun and Grant's flight engaged them. Two of the Fokkers dived past the outnumbered Americans and went after Luke, but Wehner, alert for his friend, broke away from the flight and went after the two, taking on the same two-to-one odds that he left his comrades to face. Wehner destroyed one of the Germans and the other one panicked, streaking away

U. S. Signal Corps

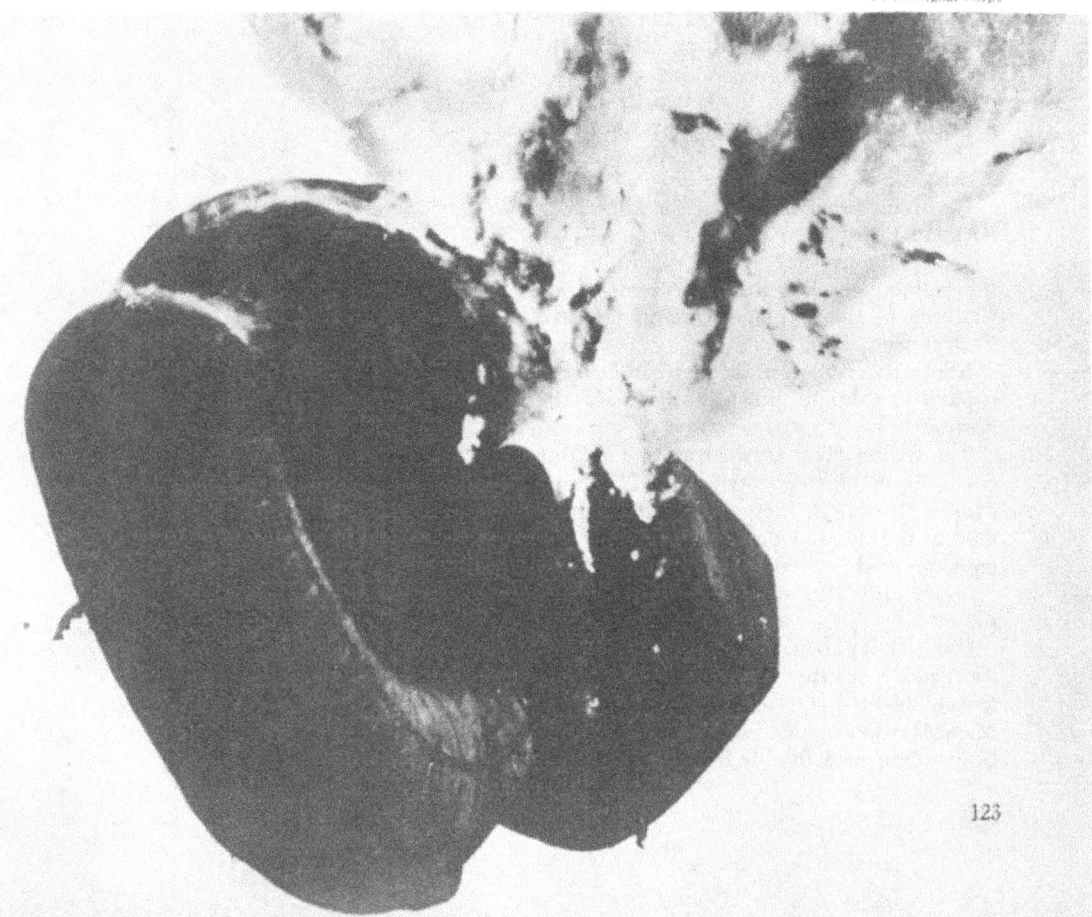

toward the auxiliary balloon drome. Luke, too, was racing away with, as he reported later, a jammed gun.

There was another balloon near Boinville and Luke, with his gun stoppage cleared, attacked it. He had to dive on it six times before he finally drove it down collapsed but not on fire.

Luke still had no technique for attacking balloons. He flew right into them through the hottest ring of the defenses, trusting to luck and serenely confident that his luck would hold. One idea did come to him, the same idea that Belgian ace Willy Coppens had exploited.

"How about catching those bags at dusk when they haul them down?" Luke said to Wehner. "I'll bet that half those guys on the guns will be having a beer or something. We could land okay if they set out flares on the drome."

On the evening of September 16, Eddie Rickenbacker was crossing the drome with two other pilots. Luke, followed by Wehner, was walking out to his ship. He stopped Rickenbacker and pointed to the eastern sky.

"Keep your eyes on those two Kraut balloons," he said. "You'll see the first one go up in flames at exactly 7:15 and the other at 7:19."

He strode away and one of the pilots with Rick laughed. "Nutty as a squirrel," he said.

The balloons were barely discernible in the fading light but the three pilots stood watching as Luke's plane took off followed by Wehner's.

At exactly 7:15 one of the German balloons exploded, a bright burst of flame on the horizon.

The second hand crawled around its tiny circle. Seven-nineteen arrived and nothing happened. At 7:20 there was another bright flash in the east and the second German balloon vanished.

"My Lord!" Rickenbacker said. "He did it."

Nor was Rickenbacker the only one who watched the sky that evening. Luke had had to confide his plans to Captain Grant and Major Hartney in order to have flares lighting the landing field for his return. By chance,

Colonel Billy Mitchell, chief of the air service, was a visitor to the field and a witness to the blazing of the balloons.

Luke, full of his triumph, came home. He had shown them. He had called his shots. Let somebody else do that!

Wehner was slower in returning. There were two more balloons beyond those that Luke got, and Wehner was caught up in the excitement of this balloon adventure. He shot them one after the other as they were being hauled down and blazed them into their nests. He didn't have anyone upstairs when he did it because Luke never gave a thought to Joe Wehner once his job was done. Men crowded around Wehner and slapped him on the back but they were too tired to really celebrate all over again. Joe Wehner had to take what was left.

Wehner, however, was thoughtful. He did not believe that a dusk raid would work twice

German Official copied by National Archives

in a row because the Germans would be expecting it; yet he knew that Luke, hot with accomplishment, would not stop now. He wanted more balloons. When Luke proposed another dusk raid on the eighteenth, Wehner shook his head.

"Let's fool them," he said. "Let's start earlier and let's both go down at the same time. We haven't tried that yet."

The two men took off at 4:00 p.m. There were two balloons near Labeuville and nice cloud cover above. Diving down on either side, Luke and Wehner set the first one afire before the protecting guns got into full action; a complete surprise attack and the easiest balloon yet. The second was tougher because the fire was heavier, but with two Spads firing into it from opposite sides the big bag went fast. The luck of the Americans held. Their planes were hit in dozens of places but not in a vital spot.

There was another balloon at St. Hilaire and they made for it. High in the sky to the east was a flight of Fokkers. Wehner signaled to Luke that he would stay above flying protection. Luke went down. He had to make three passes before the balloon exploded and he was half-blinded by the smoke. There was another balloon to the north. Could he make it four? What a day that would be!

He turned toward the other balloon, forgetting all about the Fokkers.

Wehner, upstairs, fired a signal light that Luke didn't see. Going for another balloon was madness. Six Fokkers were diving down and if Luke turned south and west away from the balloons he had a chance. When Luke turned north, the Fokkers were between the two Americans. Wehner, unhesitatingly, followed Luke, diving on the Fokkers and separating them.

Three of the Fokkers pulled up to engage

When an attacking plane came down the balloon observer got out as this German (left) demonstrates. Many pilots who lacked the guts to get a balloon, harassed the observer by feinting attack just to make him jump.

A German under attack got away before his balloon flamed as the photo (right) shows. The balloon observer's parachute was too bulky and awkward for use in airplanes; it set a man down with a bad teeth-rattling thud.

German— source unknown

FRANK LUKE

Wehner who had had no time to maneuver for a surprise attack or for advantage; the other three continued down. Luke, suddenly aware of his danger, abandoned his plan for another balloon. He met the diving Fokkers in a climbing turn and shot the leader down with a single burst, the two planes almost colliding. One of the other Fokkers yawed badly in coming out of his dive and Luke dropped on him, blasting him with incendiary bullets and sending him down in flames.

Joe Wehner, forced to change his plans too abruptly and attacking superior numbers in desperate haste, was carried too far in his dive and one of the Germans, looping out of his own dive, got on his tail. Wehner went spinning down behind the German lines with three bullets in his body.

Luke did not see him go. Having fought his way clear of his attackers, he headed for home. He saw a flight of Spads in the air, his friends, *Les Cigognes.* They were chasing a German Halberstadt which had a long lead on them. Luke, closer to the German than they were, went down on it. He fired a burst past the pilot's cockpit into the space between pilot and observer. He had balloon ammunition in his guns and the German plane blazed, rolling over slowly and plunging to earth with a long trail of black smoke.

Hour of glory and grief: Luke is standing beside the wreckage of the Halberstadt that fell under his guns as his fifth victim in a single day, Sept. 18, 1918. The photograph was taken after he had downed two balloons, two Fokkers and the two-seater shown. When he posed for the picture, Luke was not yet certain that his comrade, Lt. Joe Wehner, had been killed, but he had every reason to believe it was so.

U. S. Signal Corps

Two balloons, two Fokkers and a German observation plane in less than half an hour!

While Frank Luke was accepting congratulations from his awed fellow pilots, Joe Wehner was dying in a German field hospital.

There have been many sentimental stories written about Frank Luke's grief for Joe Wehner and his vows of vengeance, but the facts do not bear out the legends. With his five victories in one day, he received three delayed confirmations. His official score was posted at 14, twice the score of Eddie Rickenbacker. He was America's ace of aces, top man on the tally sheet.

With Luke, Squadron 27 rose to glory. It passed all other American pursuit squadrons in total victories, and it owed its pre-eminence to the man who had been the squadron dub only one week earlier.

The officers of the First Pursuit Group gave a dinner in Luke's honor on September 19, the day after his five victories and Joe Wehner's death. In the only available account of that dinner, Rickenbacker states: "He (Luke) got up laughing, said that he was having a bully time and sat down."

It could hardly have been otherwise. Luke was at the top of his game, perched on a dizzy height of adulation, and he would have been less than human if he had not reacted happily. Joe Wehner was not mentioned. Luke's last salute to him, and probably all that he could do, was the honest statement in his combat report that Joe Wehner had shared in the destruction of two of the balloons on the eighteenth and was entitled to equal credit. That credit gave Wehner a total of eight victories and placed him ahead of Rickenbacker, too, second only to Luke whose fame he had helped create.

Luke was more cocky and arrogant than ever and went to Captain Grant with a demand. He wanted a flight to protect him while he got balloons.

"Nobody has told this squadron to knock down every balloon on the front," Grant said patiently. "Some of those German balloons are wasting time observing where there's nothing to observe. Some of them are seeing what we want them to see. If we're ordered to remove a balloon and you want it, you can have it. Till then we have all our regular squadron duties to take care of."

Luke was furious. He wanted balloons but he had learned the value of top protection with Joe Wehner. There was a young pilot in the squadron, Ivan Roberts, who had gone out of his way to show his great admiration for Frank Luke. Luke sought him out.

"Want to take care of my top while I get a balloon?" he asked casually.

"Oh, boy! Do I!"

Roberts was almost speechless with excitement, visualizing himself perhaps as the successor to Joe Wehner. He went out with Luke and the two men took off. They never reached the balloon line. Five Fokkers jumped them and in the ensuing fight Luke shot one of the Fokkers down. He did not know what happened to Roberts.

Roberts was shot down behind the German lines and, according to a report, killed while trying to escape from a German prison camp.

Luke returned to the drome and took off for the nearest town without reporting in or telling anyone where he was going. He did not come back until the next day.

The irony of that episode is that corps phoned frantically to squadron shortly after Luke went AWOL, asking that a certain balloon be eliminated. Grant looked for Luke and, when no one knew where he was, Grant passed the job on to Jerry Vasconcelles.

Luke came home the following day to a reprimand from an angry Captain Grant and to the news that Jerry Vasconcelles had got a balloon in his absence. He took off in his Spad without filing a flight plan and attacked a partially inflated balloon at Bantheville, burning it in its nest.

"You're acting like a child, Luke," Grant told him. "Take 24 hours on the ground and think it over. That's an order."

Orders meant nothing to Frank Luke. He stalked out to the line and ordered his Spad warmed up. When he was told that it would have to be fueled, he was impatient.

"I'll get fuel at Vasconcelles' drome," he said.

He flew to the auxiliary drome near Verdun, but Grant, who heard his ship take off and who learned its destination from the mechanics, was ahead of him with a phone call.

"When Luke lands, place him under arrest, Jerry," he said. "I'm going to court-martial the so-and-so."

Luke landed and Vasconcelles was waiting for him. Luke knew from the flight leader's expression that he was in for trouble, but he blurted out his request for petrol.

"No dice, Frank," Vasconcelles said. "You're under arrest."

Just then a Sopwith Camel landed noisily and the pilot left the cockpit cursing fluently. Major Harold E. Hartney, on a visit to another group, had had a bad landing with his Spad and had borrowed a Camel for the return trip. The Camel had given him a lot of trouble and he chose to land at the auxiliary field rather than proceed to the home drome. Luke saw his opportunity and he took it. He reached the commander of the First Pursuit Group before Vasconcelles.

"Major," he said, "You're in time for a show. There are three balloons along the Meuse near Dun. I'll get all three, if you'll authorize the petrol."

Major Hartney brightened, forgetting his feud with the Camel. He looked upward, then at his watch. It was five after five. "Too early," he said. "Sunset is 5:22. Get 'em in the dusk. Sure you can get them?"

"Positive."

Luke looked young and confident. Major Hartney turned and ordered two mechanics

U. S. Army Air Corps

The rare photograph at left shows a flaming balloon plunging to earth.

Maj. Harold E. Hartney, commander of the First Pursuit Group, with Capt. Cunningham, his operations officer (left to right). Maj. Hartney repeatedly forgave Luke's breaches of discipline and insubordination, saving him from court-martial proceedings.

to service Luke's Spad. Jerry Vasconcelles had a problem. Technically, Luke was under arrest, but Captain Grant had not given him any details of the charge over the phone and Vasconcelles knew that Luke habitually needled and infuriated Grant. The arrest order might have arisen out of a minor matter, something that would blow over when Grant's anger cooled. On the other hand, here was Major Hartney taking over responsibility by ordering fuel for Luke.

Vasconcelles shrugged and kept silent.

Frank Luke took off at 5:22 and Major Hartney risked another flight in the balky Camel to be aloft when the first balloon flamed. Luke, with his usual concern for confirmations and hunger for an audience, streaked low over the American balloon headquarters at Souilly and dropped a message in a cylinder.

WATCH THREE HUN BALLOONS
ON MEUSE. LUKE

He was perfectly confident as always, calling his shots. He dived on the first balloon at Dun and blazed it on the first pass. Zooming out of the heavy fire, he headed for Brière and the second balloon of three. He lifted his nose, tilted his wing and went down. The ground guns opened up, but he got the balloon.

The distant watchers, Hartney in his

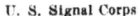
U. S. Signal Corps

Camel and the balloon observers at Souilly, saw the two bursts of flame against the sky and waited breathlessly for the third. There was a time interval, minutes of suspense, and then another tower of flame shot upward.

The observers saw no more than that. The last act was witnessed by 14 French citizens of Murvaux who told their story later and signed an affidavit.

Luke's plane was badly punished in getting that third balloon, perhaps in getting the second. He may have been hit himself. He was flying erratically when he emerged from the smoke of the third balloon and five Fokkers from an auxiliary field closed in on him. His Spad wouldn't climb and he fought with his attackers close to the ground and, apparently, shot down two of them on the outskirts of Murvaux. It was twilight and the other three Germans climbed, refusing the risk of following him into the trees, wires, a church steeple and the other hazards of a town. Luke in his Spad careened onward, flying just above the roofs and over the town's main street.

German soldiers ran out into the road and Luke did what he had never done before. He opened up with his guns on ground troops, killing 11 of them, wounding and scattering others. The Spad sank lower and lower, then veered to the right and settled into a field beyond the town limits. Luke left the cockpit and staggered over to a stream where he drank water. The Germans were running toward him and a noncom called out to him that he was a prisoner.

Luke straightened, drew an army automatic and shot the noncom dead. He continued to fire at the astonished Germans and dropped two others before one soldier raised a rifle to his shoulder and fired. Luke, hit in the chest, fell forward dropping his gun.

Frank Luke's story ended there. He died fighting on the ground when his wings would no longer support him. His enemies saw no glory in his death and they accorded him no respect. He had machine gunned their comrades with explosive bullets and such a bullet makes a horrible wound. Stripping the identification tags from his body, an officer ordered two French peasants to bury him. His grave was unmarked and the usual courtesy of notifying his countrymen was omitted.

The full story was not revealed until a graves registration detail visited Murvaux after the war and took testimony from the inhabitants.

Captain Al Grant recommended the man whom he would have court-martialed for the Congressional Medal of Honor and it was awarded posthumously.

The matter of Luke's final score has always been puzzling. At the height of his balloon streak he was granted confirmation for that first doubtful victory claim that he made although there was no more evidence to confirm it later than there had been earlier. Counting that victory, Frank Luke had 18 victories, 14 balloons and four planes, second only to Eddie Rickenbacker who had 26. In some accounts, Luke has been credited with 20 victories by adding the two Fokkers to the three balloons of his last day.

Whatever his score, Frank Luke is unique in aerial warfare, the most spectacular of the American aces. Other pilots destroyed more balloons, but no one destroyed so many in so short a time. Then, too, Frank Luke was, unlike the others, a rebel to the last. •

National Archives

Jerry Vasconcelles (left) had an order to arrest Luke when he took off on his last mission. Hartney intervened, and Luke flew to his last victories and his death. Vasconcelles, a great flight leader, was credited with seven victories at war's end. He understood Luke's problem.

Elliott White Springs
The War Bird Who'll Never Die

By William E. Barrett

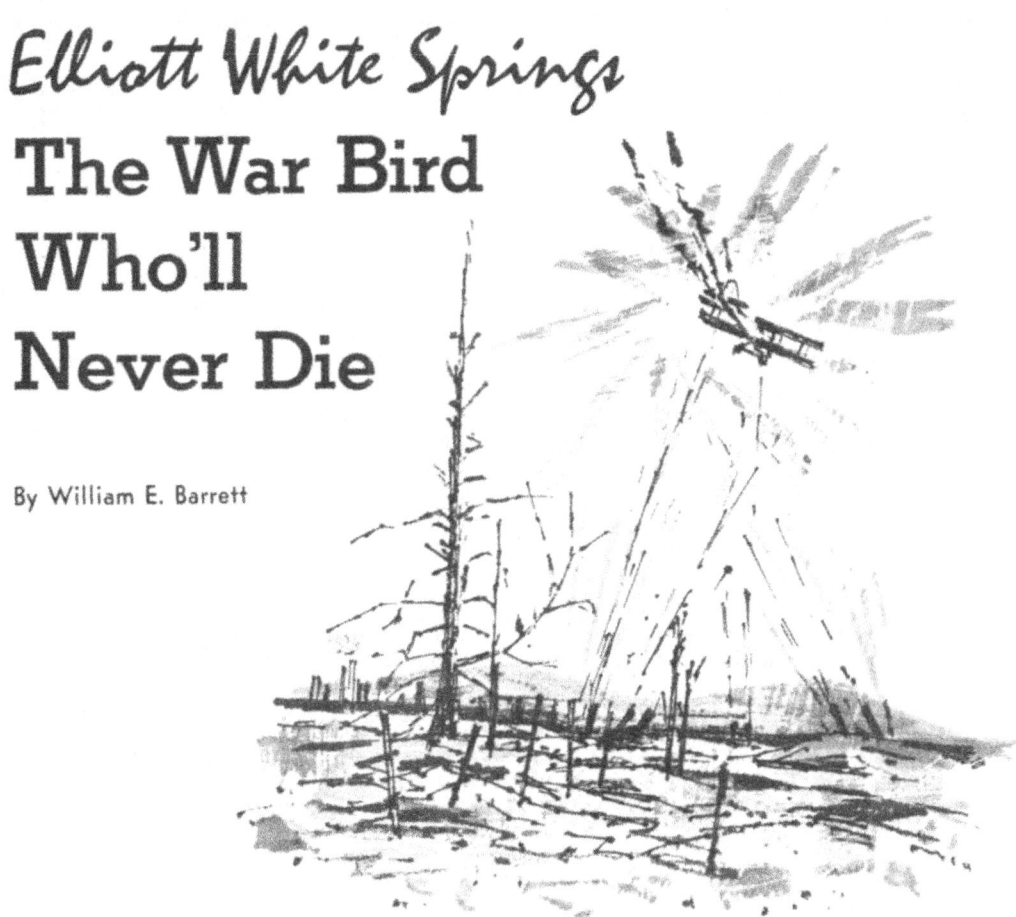

A good many people laughed when they read the obituaries which had as a subject the exploits of Elliott White Springs who died on October 15, 1959. A shocking insult to the memory of America's fifth ranking ace of World War I? No, it was not an insult. It was a compliment, for that was the way Springs would have wanted it...

THERE WAS swagger and color and daring to Elliott White Springs, and so many contradictions in his character that even his closest friends forever doubted that they understood him. To some he was a glory hunter always calling attention to himself by performing even the most routine duty spectacularly, a grandstand player, a show-off. Men who served with him deny this emphatically.

"If Springs cared for credit and claimed every German that he downed he would have been right up there with Rickenbacker," one of them said. "It was difficult to establish victory claims on the British front, under the British system, and Springs just didn't care enough to bother."

Springs never cared enough, seemingly, to worry about the opinions of other people. He took life as he found it and enjoyed what he found. He played so enthusiastically when he played that many people refused to believe that he was ever anything but a playboy. But he didn't always play. He saw so many of his friends die that he developed a defense against any betrayal of emotion and refused to sentimentalize friendship and parting and death. To many, therefore, he was without loyalty or deep feeling.

He trained for air warfare in England during a time of great tension and "war nerves" when liquor provided a means of escape from grim realities, but Springs did not consider sodden unconsciousness an escape. He invented weird and wonderful drinks and christened them with preposterous names. He mixed alcohol with humor and produced a certain cockeyed gaiety which won him a reputation as an amateur bartender and a great party spark plug. To many that reputation outlived his solid achievements and one article about him was titled *The Cocktail Ace*.

But his friends didn't buy that title. "He did a lot of serious drinking," one of them said, "but he never took liquor seriously."

Springs was one of the most colorful survivors of the mad air world of 1917-18 and he is still a contradiction and a puzzle, criticized and defended as hotly today as he was when he was recklessly young and touched with a certain invincibility.

When the United States entered World War I in April 1917, Elliott White Springs was 20 years old and a student at Princeton. In every way he was a southern gentleman descended from southern gentlemen. He had prepared for Princeton at Culver, famous for its Black Horse Troop. He was handsome, literary and lazily athletic. He wrote poetry. No one would have looked at him and guessed that he was tough.

But tough he was, inside and out. He had grown up with the conviction that if he failed at anything that he attempted he would not only be failing himself but those who believed in him. It was a difficult load to carry on young shoulders. His father, Colonel Leroy

Elliott White Springs and his flight: Members of B flight of the 148th Squadron, U.S.A.S., are, from left to right, Lt. P. E. Cunnius, Lt. S. Q. Noel, Lt. E. W. Springs, Commander, Lt. L. K. Callahan, Lt. O. A. Ralston and Lt. Harry Jenkinson, Jr. Lt. Jenkinson was later killed in action.

U. S. Signal Corps

Springs, wrote letters, well-meaning letters that impressed upon his son the fact that he expected great things of him. Colonel Springs wrote without humor and his son considered the letters a burden. Elliott developed an aversion to the doing of great things. His father seemed to have the idea that he should be a good young acorn and grow into a sturdy oak. Elliott White Springs didn't have time for that.

Princeton men were leaving college for the navy in the spring and summer of 1917, or drilling on the campus in preparation for entering the army. Others were attracted to the flying school which Princeton alumni planned to finance. Elliott White Springs was the first man to sign up when the flight training project became a reality in June.

He spent two months in ground school studying theory of flight at Princeton, then shipped to Mineola, Long Island, with the rank of sergeant. A number of partly-informed and misinformed young men were gathered there from all over the country, eager to climb into cockpits and darken the skies over Europe as the politicians had promised. There were no cockpits. Instead of learning to fly, they studied Italian. The United States was establishing a flying field at Foggia, Italy, where they could all be trained.

Though Springs still wore the marks of Princeton he was now wearing a sergeant's stripes and this meant responsibility. To his surprise he found that very few of this air-minded mob at Mineola knew as much about a military organization as did the plebe class at Culver. He did not know how much authority he had over a bunch of strangers, but the strangers didn't know either. So he gave orders and they were obeyed; and he arranged complicated matters that stayed arranged—and thoroughly enjoyed himself.

He was wary of all the brand-new officers of a brand-new army until he discovered that they were afraid of a sergeant who acted as though he knew his way around. When one of them interfered with any of his projects or arrangements, he politely but firmly quoted rule 115 or 124 of an imaginary manual to support his position and watched, poker-faced, while the officer's assurance melted into weak acquiescence.

By the time the unwieldy rookie group marched aboard the *Carmania* for overseas, Springs was a top sergeant with almost as much authority as a colonel.

Among his group was a husky youngster from Arkansas named John McGavock Grider who would later play a large role in Springs' life.

Right then Grider had a problem. Larry Callahan, his roommate at the Champaign, Illinois ground school, was assigned to the French study group bound for France while he was studying Italian and would probably go to Italy. That was a high-level problem, far beyond an ordinary sergeant's sphere. But Springs requisitioned Callahan out of the French group and got away with it.

That was the tip-off on Springs who would tackle anything whether it was in the book or not. It was also the beginning of a Three Musketeers association though none of the three men realized it at the time.

The *Carmania* sailed from New York on September 17, 1917 and waited in Halifax for a convoy. On a long, slow journey across, the 150 young men who dreamed of glory in the air were busy with their speeded-up courses in Italian. Most of them had shipped baggage and personal effects to Italy. They landed in England on October 2 and found this was not a stopover; it was the end of the line. Someone had changed orders on them. They were to be trained in England by the English.

The English had planned for them as little as they had planned for the English. England was fighting a very grim war in France and training pilots to replace those who were being killed daily over the lines. There were no training facilities for 150 Americans who could not be provided with planes by their own government once they were trained. They went to Oxford for more ground school and here the genius of Springs showed itself immediately. The Americans had to live under American regulations but under British command, and it took a top sergeant with imagination to find a middle path which would make life tolerable.

To do this Springs acted as a buffer between the command and the commanded and, at the same time, became the best party organizer in England.

ELLIOTT WHITE SPRINGS

He was one of the first to move out of the eternal ground school and on to flight training. Once he had discovered how it was done, he arranged for Grider and Callahan to follow him. They trained on ancient arks like the Farman, graduated to Avros and went on to Sopwith Pups; three men who, remarkably, had the same aptitudes for flying, the same feel for the air; the qualities of good pursuit pilots. They started together and they stayed together. Many of their friends died in training planes and they became accustomed to funerals.

With the English flying schools behind them, the three moved on to Turnbery in Scotland where they learned the arts of gunnery and practiced combat flying. Here Springs received his commission as a first lieutenant on March 25, 1918. Grider and Callahan were commissioned on April 1. Even if only by a step or two or a day or two, Springs always managed to establish seniority and command; it was born in him.

With the two other Musketeers, Springs went back to London to await orders. London was a big adventure for young officers with wings. There were parties and dances, girls, shows, clubs that were gay all night. Most people liked the newcomers—but there were exceptions. One night in a bar, a tall, lean British guardsman showed his dislike. "The Yanks do a good show," he said, "drinking and playing in London, but they won't fight."

Elliott White Springs laid down his glass. He still looked like a college boy in uniform and the guardsman towered over him.

U. S. Signal Corps

"You're all wrong, soldier," he said quietly. "Here's one that will."

The guardsman doubled his fists and Springs caught him with a left-right combination that folded him in two and sent him crashing into a table. Two other guardsmen came into it and someone in the corner of the room threw a bottle that smashed against the bar. The three Americans did not wait to choose opponents. They hit anyone who was in the way until they reached the street. Ten minutes later they were sitting in another bar with replacements for the interrupted drinks, ignoring their bruises, talking about anything and everything but the fight.

They did not know it, but right at that time they—and all like them—were the subject of a big debate between governments.

England had trained these fighting pilots. Now, the United States was requesting that they all be held, put on ice somewhere until there were some American squadrons to which they could be assigned. England was saying "No" emphatically. Manpower was too precious to be wasted. English squadrons needed replacements, trained men. If the United States could not use these pilots that England had trained, then, dammit-all, England could.

Once more Springs' affinity for meeting and impressing people paid off. He had met the great Major Billy Bishop, the Canadian ace, at Turnbery and had introduced his two friends to him. At the time the United States reluctantly agreed to "lend" its men to the Royal Air Force, Bishop was organizing a new squadron and remembered the three Americans.

"About the middle of April, I got wind of what I considered to be a prize," Bishop wrote in his book, *Winged Warfare*—"at a training camp nearby were three Americans who had just learned to fly; Springs, Callahan and Grider were their names; they were known throughout the camp as 'the Three Musketeers,' and they had a reputation of being—all of them—wonderful pilots. In fact, the first time they flew alone, each one of them, one after the other, looped, did a spin and some other stunts which the trained pilots are accustomed to do. This, of course, made their reputation. They were anxious to go to France with my squadron—and I applied for them."

Springs and his friends had not only been "anxious to go to France" with Bishop's squadron, but with any squadron, and Springs had been playing every angle in sight. For once the Springs' smartness outsmarted itself. He got himself assigned to a Spad squadron and then pulled wires for his friends. Only one more pilot was needed after Springs and Callahan made it, leaving Grider out. Springs was stunned, but he assured Grider that he would fix it up for him as soon as he reported. He reported to the Spad squadron and a shock awaited him. Major Raikes, the commanding officer, was coldly formal.

"I have a report that you are not qualified to fly Spads," he said. "So, I am sending you back."

The usual Springs resourcefulness deserted

More "War Birds:" This is A flight of the 148th Squadron. From left to right are Lt. L. T. Wyly, Lt. Louis W. Rabe, Lt. Field Kindley, Commander, Lt. Walter B. Knox and Lt. Jesse O. Creech. Field Kindley is holding "Fokker," the mascot of the flight.

him. "I do fly Spads," he said hotly. "I have flown Spads. I'll fly any Spad you've got."

Raikes read from the report on his desk and the more Springs argued, the less he convinced Raikes. It was one of his rare failures and he went back, vowing that there would be an inquiry on the source of such an irresponsible report. He did not discover for several days that the joke was on him and that he had received the break of his life.

Major Bishop, seeking "the Three Musketeers" for his newly-formed 85th Squadron, had missed Springs by a half-hour and had faked the report which went to Raikes. He caught Callahan, too, before Callahan was accepted by the Spad squadron.

Life had a special flavor for Springs and his companions after that. They were no longer unattached, no longer orphans of war. They belonged definitely to a war-bound squadron—the 85th—flying the ship in which they would fight, the S.E. 5. They flew and practiced combat with one another every day and they enjoyed London to the full at night. They honored every rumor that they were going over "tomorrow" with a farewell party and they lived each hour to the hilt.

On May 22, 1918 they flew across the channel to France.

There was no squadron in the R.A.F. more cosmopolitan than 85. It had six pilots from Canada, two from Australia, two from New Zealand, two from Scotland, one from Ireland, one from South Africa, six from England and three from the United States. They took off from England in glory with their girl friends seeing them off, and they discovered when they reached their assigned drome at Petit-Synthe that there was a war and that they were in it. They had to put their ships in hangars with no ground crew to help them and when they went wearily to their quarters, they discovered that there were no lights. What was worse, there were no blankets and no place to sleep except the bare floors.

It took two weeks to organize the squadron, to get all the ships and guns in fighting trim— two weeks in which the pilots flew short patrols but were not allowed to approach the front lines. Major Bishop was uncompromisingly strict on this point and Springs, more than any of the others, rebelled at what he considered an overcautious attitude on the part of the commander. Springs, for all of the maturing experience he had had, was still a reckless romantic not only dreaming of adventure but seeking it.

As was to be expected, Bishop did not stay away from the front lines for two weeks himself. On May 29, exactly one week after the 85th reached Petit-Synthe, he went out on a solo patrol and shot down a two-seater near Ypres. He got two more three days later.

This was all too much for the impatient Springs. On the morning of June 4 he took off alone in his S.E. and headed for the front lines. He had dreams of doing as Bishop had done and he looked for a German two-seater as he neared the lines. Some German hunters found him before he found a German. Six Pfalz dived on him and he did not see them until splinters flew past his face and holes appeared magically in his wings.

Springs, the casual, the debonair, the unruffled, met fear in that moment. Death was split seconds and fractional inches away from him and he knew that he did not have a chance in a battle with six Germans. He forgot all that he had learned and did the wrong thing, the normally fatal thing. He dived away full gun from the enemy.

He should have died there over Courtrai, but he didn't. The Germans, perhaps, were startled by a pilot who flew alone doing such a stupid thing.

Springs, plunging down at a long slant across the lines, had other worries besides the Germans. The linen of his top plane, riddled by bullets, was stripping off in ribbons as he dived. When he pulled out of his dive the S.E. tried to spin and it took all that he had learned in many hours of flying to hold it level. He came in over the drome at Petit-Synthe wanting nothing so much as the feeling of solid ground under him, and he landed too hot. The S.E. bounced, then ground-looped and crashed into the private and personal S.E. 5 of Major William A. Bishop, V. C.

Bishop himself, surrounded by a half dozen pilots, was standing grimly on the apron when Springs extricated himself from the wreckage. It was the worst moment of Springs' young life. He had disobeyed orders, had taken an awful licking from the Germans whom he was so anxious to fight, and he had destroyed

THE WAR BIRD WHO'LL NEVER DIE

two S.E.s after flying home with death riding beside him in the cockpit. He was shaken and more than a little sick, but the peculiar genius that had made him a leader wherever he went had not deserted him. He should have been abject and apologetic, but he wasn't. He walked up to the great Bishop and ran his fingers across the rows of ribbons on the commanding officer's tunic.

"See those decorations?" he asked hoarsely. "Well, you're welcome to them."

He walked away then and Bishop was too surprised to call him back. In his own quarters, Springs fought a lonely battle with his pride. He was wrong and he knew it. He had failed himself when he disobeyed orders and in failing himself he had failed others who had confidence in him. Obeying a reckless impulse he had very nearly thrown away his life, wasted the training that had been given him and compromised the squadron commander who was responsible for him. Springs faced himself and later that night he faced Bishop. He walked into the Major's quarters and apologized.

The next day Bishop led a six-man flight, which included Springs, on a patrol in the Courtrai area where Springs had encountered the six Pfalz. The methodical Germans were flying the same patrol area; six black Pfalz in two layers of three planes each. Bishop had briefed his men on what to do if they en-

There's a grin on Springs' face despite the fact that he's just cracked up this Sop Camel.

countered the Germans and there was no hesitation when he gave the signal. They split into two flights themselves and went down.

The Germans never knew what hit them. Bishop, MacGregor and Springs shot down a Pfalz each in that first swift assault. The other three rolled under the attack and spun down. Bishop signaled the wash-out and let them go.

Springs was jubilant. Yesterday's humiliation had been wiped out in an instant. He had scored a victory in the air. He had destroyed one of the Germans who had shot him up and chased him home. He was singing in the cockpit as he flew back to the drome. He came in over the tracks at the edge of the field and there was a train on the siding. He was thinking of his victory and his approach was low. He lifted the nose of the S.E. 5, just barely clearing the tops of the boxcars, and plowed into the field, nose-down. He had learned in flying school that a glide cannot be stretched. This made it official.

For the second time in two days he crawled out of the wreckage of an S.E. on his own drome and again Bishop was waiting for him.

U. S. Signal Corps

"Well, you've destroyed three of our planes and only one German so far," Bishop said. "Which side are you on?"

For once Springs was without a comeback. His mood had soared too high and fallen too low, and he was humbled. It would take only two more washed-out S.E.s to make him a German ace.

Right after that 85 Squadron drew the uninspiring job of escorting the D.H. 9 bombers of 311 Squadron which bombed the submarine bases at Zeebrugge every morning. It was dangerous work because the antiaircraft fire was heavy, but there were no combats. Some of the pilots of the "nines" were Americans too. There were 216 American pilots trained in English schools and serving in British squadrons under British officers, a lost legion as far as their own country was concerned. The American training center at Issoudun, France, was highly publicized at home. Articles were written about it and motion pictures taken of the training and of the men trained there. Newspaper correspondents followed the graduates of Issoudun into the newly formed American squadrons while the men who were first across, who were trained and ready before America had any squadrons in which to use them, were ignored.

The Germans were staging their last great offensive of the war in June. They had one chance, and one chance only, to destroy the British and the French armies and to force a negotiated peace before the full weight of American men and equipment made itself felt.

They knew it and they went all out.

Eighty-Five Squadron was transferred to St. Omer on the hottest front where the Germans had concentrated two-seaters for observation and fighting scouts to protect them. There were combats on every patrol from the drome at St. Omer and Bishop ran up the record score of the war in the first 12 days—25 German planes destroyed. No other ace had ever scored so many victories in so short a time.

On June 18, Springs went out on a volun-

Elliott White Springs about to start out on a patrol in his Sopwith Camel and defying the superstition that no pilot should have his picture taken before taking off on a war mission.

tary patrol with "Mac" Grider. It was a day of gloom, of dark, heavy clouds hanging low and they seemed to be alone in the sky. They crossed the lines and flew deep into German air. Suddenly they saw a German two-seater beneath them, one of the older types, an Albatros. The crew spotted them as they came down and raced away. Over Armentières the two Southerners caught up with their quarry. Springs came down on top, shooting at the pilot, while Grider dived past the two-seater and zoomed up under the blind spot. Both men were firing when the Albatros burst into flames and went spinning down.

It had been a quick victory. Springs and Grider were satisfied. They exchanged signals and headed for home, racing in and out of the valleys between towering mountains of cloud, Springs leading as he always did. Halfway home Springs missed Grider. He turned back and circled, looking for the other S.E., but the sky was as lonely as a landscape of the moon. He gave up ultimately convinced that Grider had somehow gotten ahead of him. He had flown with Grider too often to be worried. "Mac" could take care of himself in the air and today there was no menace, nothing to worry anyone.

Springs landed at St. Omer and Grider had not come back. John McGavock Grider never did come back. Like many other airmen of the war, he vanished, leaving not even a body as evidence that he had ever existed.

For days, Springs and Callahan kept a vigil, refusing to concede the fact that the third Musketeer was gone. Then the hope gradually died.

The last part of Elliott White Springs, the college boy embarked on high adventure, died when "Mac" Grider died. He had been doing a man's work for a year, of course, and taking a man's risks, but he had been gay through most of it.

Now he turned to the grim job of sorting out a dead man's personal effects and packing them to be sent home. One was always careful not to send a wrong letter home, a wrong souvenir, anything which might hurt someone who would not understand.

Grider had kept a diary. Springs had never read it but he did it now, and marveled at how good it was, how truthfully it portrayed the life that they had led, the history of that lost legion that started out to be trained in Foggia and had ended up in England. It was good, too good. There might be hurt or worry in it for some people, Grider's own or the families of men he mentioned. Springs conferred with Larry Callahan and decided not to send the diary home.

The diary of John McGavock Grider was to be the foundation of the most famous of all war flying narratives—*War Birds*. It was sketchy and there were many days with no entries but the entries themselves were starkly dramatic. Later when he came to edit it, Springs realized its essential weakness; that, like Grider's life, too much of the diary was devoted to the long preparation for action, action that was tragically short. So, some of the diary came out and many of Spring's own notes and observations went in. Instead of ending the narrative on June 18 when Grider died, Springs extended it to the end of August. When he released it for publication years later he conceived of it as the diary of many men rather than of one; a memorial to "Mac" who remained anonymous to all except those who had shared the adventure with him. The royalties went to finance a project that Grider had planned. Springs touched none of them.

On June 21, Bishop left 85 Squadron. He was called home to organize the Royal Canadian Air Force. Captain Baker became acting squadron commander, with Springs taking over command of Baker's flight.

There was a new, grim element in Springs' attitude toward the war now. On June 23, his first day as flight leader, he blasted a Pfalz scout out of the air over the Menin Road. The following day he shot down an L. V. G. in the same area. He was restless and often flew voluntary patrols alone as if, like so many others who lost friends, he was torn by the feeling that "I might have saved him if I had kept closer watch over him." Ridiculous, of course, but human. On two of these solo patrols Springs destroyed German planes over German territory without the necessary confirmation to make them official.

On June 27 Springs was flying with Inglis and MacGregor over the Armentières area where he had lost Grider. They spotted a German two-seater and went down on it. This

ELLIOTT WHITE SPRINGS

German was a Hannoveranner and a very tough foe—powerful, maneuverable, armored and equipped with a gun tunnel on the underside to eliminate the blind spot. Inglis drew the assignment of attacking the pilot while Springs took the rear gunner from the underside and MacGregor took him from the rear.

MacGregor yawed badly as he came out of his dive under the German's fire and fell off in a spin. The German pilot zoomed to get a shot at Inglis, and Springs, coming up from beneath the big ship, got the full fire of the rear guns. Suddenly Springs' own gun ceased to function and hot oil from a punctured line spurted into his face. Temporarily blinded, he spun down. As he did, he whipped off his oil-spattered goggles, remembering that he was behind the German lines, aware that his ship was crippled.

It looked like the end of the war. The bearings of the oil-less Hispano-Suiza engine froze up as Springs leveled off with his nose pointed toward his own lines. Dead stick he glided across the German positions as antiaircraft gunners and riflemen poured fire at him.

The ground was coming up at him fast and he could not maneuver or pick his landing place. No Man's Land was wide and he had to get as close to his own lines as he could. A sandbag protected machine gun nest loomed up ahead of him and he hit.

The butt of the Vickers gun smashed Springs in the mouth and the S.E. broke up all around him, tearing at his clothing, raking his flesh. The light of the world flickered and went out.

He came back to consciousness on the floor of a trench with a couple of British Tommies working on him. His mouth was ablaze and he could taste his own blood. When he sought for his teeth with his tongue, there were no

Three for tea: The men who trained with Springs were scattered through many British squadrons because the U.S.A.S. was not ready to absorb them. The Yanks in the photo belonged to 84 Squadron, R.A.F. The pilot without a tunic and his back to his S.E. 5 is George A. Vaughn, credited with 12 enemy aircraft destroyed and one balloon. He flew Camels with 17 Squadron, U.S.A.S., after transferring from the R.A.F. He, Springs and others who went to war early were unknown "orphans."

U. S. Signal Corps

teeth. One of the Tommies gripped his lips and pulled on it. Springs almost passed out again, but his teeth were, miraculously, back in his mouth. He had been wearing them on the outside of his face. Two more men came with a stretcher and loaded the partly-conscious Springs onto it.

The doctors at the base hospital wanted to send him back to England, Springs learned when he came out of a coma several days later. Even though he was sick and groggy, he didn't want that. He had an idea that the war needed him.

On July 2, he escaped from the hospital and made his way back to his squadron in pajamas—to discover that he had been appointed flight commander in a new American squadron, the 148th, equipped with Sopwith Camels.

The United States was then in the process of reclaiming some of their best pilots from the British, but Springs did not believe that the Americans knew how to run an air force as the British did. He had nothing in common with the men who had trained at Issoudun or the men who had won promotions in the States before coming overseas. He had served under British officers who could not promote him because he was an American but who understood him and accepted him for what he could do. He had no liking for the Sopwith Camel, either, after flying S.E. 5s. Of course, he could still return to the hospital. But that meant returning to England.

He had another disappointment awaiting him besides the transfer that he did not want. He had been recommended for the Distinguished Flying Cross a week before he crashed into the sandbags but the recommendation had not been approved. He was officially credited with only four victories and a man had to have five to rate a D. F. C. On the American front, by American scoring methods, he was certain that he would have had ten or a dozen victories. He reacted in typical fashion.

"Hell," he said. "Why argue about it?"

He was too rocky for a farewell party so he settled for sleep on his last night in 85 Squadron. On July 3 he reported to 148 Squadron, U.S.A.S., the most thoroughly secondhand and completely beaten-up fighting man ever returned to American command by the British. His mouth was still raw, inside and out, his neck was stiff and he had a hemorrhage in the retina of one eye. The anti-tetanus serum with which they had filled him in the hospital had upset his stomach so that he could take no solid food. And the healthy, bounding, confident enthusiasm of the pilots in his new squadron made him feel like an old man.

Mort Newhall was commander of 148. Bim Oliver and Henry Clay were the other two flight leaders. Like Springs, both men had been at Oxford and had served in British squadrons. That helped.

On August 3 Springs scored the squadron's first victory; a Fokker that he shot down in flames behind his own lines. He was back to his old specialty of being first in anything that he undertook.

Larry Callahan, the famous "Cal" of *War Birds*, who trained with Springs, served with him in the R.A.F. and transferred with him to the U.S.A.S., 148 Squadron. Larry Callahan, although credited in American records with only one victory, appears on British records with eight.

U. S. Signal Corps

On August 21, death reached for him again. Outmaneuvered and out-gunned by two Fokker D-7s, he limped home with his Camel badly shot up. Though Springs didn't know it, the plane had a ruined undercarriage and one wheel had been shot away.

When he came in over the drome, he saw the mechanics running around waving wheels at him.

He slowly circled the field as he thought that one over, then made up his mind.

He came in and took the shock on one wing. The little ship cart-wheeled as it broke up then slid to a halt. Springs walked from the wreckage with only a few bruises.

The next day he was back at it again. Headquarters had sent down word that a certain German balloon across the lines was playing hell with the infantry by directing artillery fire on them. Would 148 please remove it? The three flight commanders cut cards for this ugly assignment and Springs drew the low card. His luck seemed to be running out.

Shooting down balloons was one of the tough jobs of the war, almost a suicide job, and the Camel was not designed for such work. The Camel was an adroit and acrobatic ship, a great dogfighter, but the ships that got balloons were ships of greater horsepower and sturdier construction—Spads, or S.E.s or AK.Ws. The proper procedure was to fly to the balloon as a flight and send one man down to get it. The etiquette of the situation forbade asking for volunteers—which was embarrassing—or selecting a man for the job which was too much like passing a sentence of death on a mate.

Springs summoned his flight. He had a pack of cards. Cutting for the suicide stunt was the only fair way. He fingered the pack of cards, then threw it away. Some of these kids were rookies. None of them had as much experience as he had.

"We're going out to get a damn balloon," he said evenly. "I'll go down on it, but I want you flying top protection."

Springs led his flight across the lines, miles south of his objective, then flew north, approaching the balloon from the east, the German side of the lines, with the morning sun at his back. He had to watch out for hostile flights every minute once they flew into German air. The best of the German aces liked to hunt over their own territory where confirmations of victories were easy. This morning the high blue was remarkably clear. He flew steadily west with his flight behind him and he was neither happy nor depressed, merely resigned, slightly numb, not permitting himself to think about the job that was his to do.

Far beneath him he spotted the balloon, a small gray blob when viewed from the heights, a tiny thing swaying in the breeze but seemingly fixed like a tack against the map below.

Curtiss Aeroplane Company

CURTISS JENNY—1918

A few wisps of white cloud floated between him and his objective. He drew a deep breath and wagged his wings in a signal to his flight.

A brief second, then, to search the sky, to fix his objective on the ground, and he took off; lifting the nose of his Camel, dropping one wing, lining out in swift, diving flight.

Then the gray blob was monstrous in his sights—a huge elephantine object with black crosses on its dingy fabric. Black bursts of Archy flowered below him and he saw the huge bag sway as the winch operators sought frantically to haul it down. Two parachutes snapped open, awkward umbrellas carrying the balloon crew to earth. As he fingered the trips of his guns, the black bursts were no longer below him. They were all around him. The odds were 100 to 1 against a Camel on a show like this. The antiaircraft gunners had a fixed range and could crisscross their fire above the bag. Around the base, the machine gunners were holding their fire. They, too, had accurate range.

Springs pressed the gun trips as the balloon filled his sights. Shrapnel was tearing through his wings and rough, giant fingers reached into his cockpit to pluck at his sleeve, tearing a long gash from elbow to shoulder. He held his fire steady, concentrating on the job that he had to do, pouring his phosphorous bullets into the *Drachen*. He pulled back on the stick when he was almost at the point of running into the big bag. His flying wires screamed and he could feel his ship fighting him as he pulled out of his dive. The odor of hot castor oil from the rotary engine was in his nostrils. The machine guns below were drumming.

Behind him, Springs heard a long, deep sigh, then a belching sound as the balloon burst into flames. He raced across the stuttering machine guns and headed for his own lines.

Years later, Elliott White Springs made a short story out of that day's experience, a story titled "9214" which appeared in one of the best of his books, *Above the Bright Blue Sky*. But on that hot summer day he was not thinking about stories—he was merely glad to get home.

The war went on. Squadron 148 was an American squadron but it was nearly as much an orphan as were the pilots who had transferred to it from the British. With its companion squadron, 17, it served on the British front with the British 4th Army, far away from the American newsreel cameras, the American correspondents and the American hero-makers.

On August 22 Springs was flying a solo patrol again when he sighted five Fokkers flying in close formation below him. A solitary Camel in such a circumstance was entitled to ignore the situation, but caution was not born in Springs. He tipped one wing, dropped his nose and dived on them. His guns took the rearmost Fokker out of contention before the flight knew that it was attacked and he shot down another before the Fokkers could fire a shot at him. His guns jammed then and he kept on going, out of range before his victims hit the earth.

He landed only briefly on his own drome to clear the gun stoppage and took off again. Over Bapaume there were three Fokkers worrying a poor old British R.E. 8 which should have been retired in 1916. Springs attacked as he had attacked the five Fokkers earlier, but with even greater steam, aware that the lives of the two men in the R.E. 8 depended upon him. He knocked the first Fokker into the fortifications of Bapaume for a confirmed victory, but the other two were not as easy. They chased tails with him while the prevailing wind carried them over the German lines.

Finally he succeeded in shooting both of them down without a confirmation on either.

From that day's work, in which he had destroyed five Fokkers, he returned to his drome without a single bullet hole in his wings; the first time he had ever come out of any fight unmarked.

From that point on, Springs was invincible. He was a driving, irrepressible, untiring force, a leader who, time after time, saved

Most American-trained and Canadian-trained pilots who went to war trained on the Curtiss Jenny (left), one of the greatest and certainly the most famous training ship ever built. Springs and other Americans who trained early in England missed the Jenny experience, although it was used there, too, near the war's end.

ELLIOTT WHITE SPRINGS

men of his flight from death, careless of credit or of scores in the tally sheet. Squadron 148, the squadron to which he did not want to go, became his pride. It came late to the front, three months later than the widely publicized 94th, Rickenbacker's Hat-in-the-Ring Squadron, but it had only three fewer victories than the 94th when the final shot was fired.

Squadron 148 had 66 confirmed victories in 2,100 hours of flying and suffered only 11 casualties; a ratio of six to one. In addition to aerial combat, the pilots of 148 strafed the German trenches and attacked enemy troops behind the German lines. Elliott White Springs with 12 official victories was America's fifth ranking ace and, when the war ended, commander of 148 Squadron.

The Armistice was signed, and it took a long time for a man to run down his momentum after he had lived for long months on the fast toboggan of war in the air. Springs tried to run some of that momentum out in France, later came home as a test pilot for L.F.W. Airplane Company. He then went to work for his father who controlled mills, banks and a railroad. Colonel Leroy Springs still clung to the theory that one should begin as an acorn and grow into an oak. He did not seem to understand that his son was no longer in the acorn stage.

Elliott rebelled against this treatment and launched his own career as a writer. In his books he captured faithfully the flavor of a day that was gone, the men who lived and the men who died, the play days in England, the fighting in war skies, the mad, unreasonable maladjustments to peace. He wrote with irrepressible humor, often exaggerating to the point of absurdity in order to puncture the pretentious and those who played the perpetual hero in order to capitalize on their war experiences.

In later years he was to put his typewriter away and step into the shoes of his father as a captain of industry. Never would he lose his sense of humor, his irreverent, outrageous attitude toward the conventional, the shallow, the mind of small dimensions.

Elliott White Springs will always be many things to many people. He was a show-off or he wasn't; an underrated ace or an overrated one; a mill-owning tycoon or a neighbor to those who worked for him; a scatterbrained playboy or a man of tremendous ability who refused to take his own accomplishments too seriously. The real man is somewhere between the contradictions.

But all will agree on one thing: In all his life Elliott White Springs never sent someone else down after that balloon. •

Springs scored his most notable victories in the Sopwith Camel (below) although he preferred the S.E. 5. Squadrons 17 and 148, composed of American pilots who had served with British squadrons, were Camel equipped. In his book *Nocturne Militaire* Springs wrote this description of the Sopwith Camel: "You know, a Camel was so short that it would roll of its own accord, due to the torque, and naturally a rotary motor increased and emphasized the torque. Flying a Camel was just like riding a gyroscope that was out of balance. They vibrated like a hula dancer's empennage and smelled like the inside of a motorman's mitt." Many pilots agreed.

Royal Air Force

www.ingramcontent.com/pod-product-compliance
Lightning Source LLC
LaVergne TN
LVHW061253060426
835507LV00017B/2046